MW01061519

On the Wings of Eros

On the Wings of Eros

Nightly Readings for Passion & Romance

COMPILED BY ALICIA ALVREZ

FOREWORD BY DAPHNE ROSE KINGMA

CONARI PRESS
Berkeley, California

Conari Press books are distributed by Publishers Group West

Cover: Karen Bouris and Generic Typography
Photo: Copyright © Steven Burr Williams/The Image Bank (sculpture
by Antonio Canova, *Psyche Brought Back to Life by the Kiss of Amour*)

ISBN: 1-57324-013-3

Acknowledgment of permission to reprint previously published material
can be found on pp 210–213, which constitute an extension of the
copyright page.

Library of Congress Cataloging-in-Publication Data
On the wings of Eros : nightly readings for passion & romance /
    [collected by] Alicia Alvrez.
        p.   cm.
    ISBN 1-57324-013-3
        1. Love—Literary collections.   2. Sex—Literary collections.
        I. Alvrez, Alicia.
    PN6071.L705   1995
    808.8'03538—dc20   95-20441

Printed in the United States of America

10 9 8 7 6 5 4 3 2 1

Eros, the god of love, emerged to create the earth.

Before, all was silent, bare, and motionless.

Now, all was life, joy, and motion.

EARLY GREEK MYTH

Acknowledgments

Copious thanks to Daphne Rose Kingma for writing the foreword, Judy Ford for giving me the title, Dawna Markova for suggesting good source material, and Claudia Schaab, Heather Bloch, and Vanessa Sabarese for helping with the selection process, computer input, and permission wrangling.

Nourishing Your Erotic Connection

Nothing in life, or in love, gives us more pleasure than our erotic experience, the way we physically bond, join with, caress, embrace, and inhabit one another. That's because eroticism isn't just the sexual encounter; it is sensuality in all its forms, the breathtaking (and giving) experience of the beloved, of the human being in his or her physical form. The sensual is neither isolated from love nor is it all that love is. Rather, it is the tempting, tantalizing walk on the tightrope (and free-fall through the air) between the trapezes of our ordinary lives and our most precious moments of human interaction.

Sex is joyful, deep, and healing—two bodies joining in sound and movement, in flowing, discovering, and knowing. Nothing can make you feel more "in love" than a marvelous sexual experience; nothing can revive or deepen a love grown familiar so much as an erotic renaissance, and, conversely, nothing can make you feel more discouraged about your relationship than a sexual connection gone awry. Indeed, your erotic life, more than almost anything else, can reflect the true condition of your love. It can teach you about your beloved, reach you through to the realm of your spirit, take you to the depths of your own ecstatic vulnerability.

That's why your sexual relationship, far from being dispensable, an adjunct to what we ordinarily think of as the core of our relationships—the fact that we live together or are married, share a household, children, or a checkbook—is your love's very breath and essence.

But this delicious richness is rarely nourished in our lives. Sexual and sensual pleasures are often the first thing to be sacrificed in relationships bombarded by the stresses of a busy world. Like everything else that is precious—our bodies, our children, our breath, our emotional lives, our health, and the earth we live on, the fragile yet beautiful erotic impulse must be nurtured or it will gradually abandon us.

This book is an instrument to that purpose—food for the life of the senses, nourishment for your precious erotic connection with your beloved. Charmingly, passionately, exquisitely, it walks you through the many glorious and tender vicissitudes of erotic love—exciting, cajoling, inspiring. Read it to charm and amuse yourself, to delight your senses and kindle your passion, to inspire a fine tenderness. Read it aloud to each other to renew your early days of romance, to deepen the love you have forged with time.

But above all read it with pleasure, for your erotic life is light, delight, attention, compassion, passion, excitement, tenderness, fulfillment, ecstasy; rejoicing, relief, rejuvenation, rapture, harmony, lust, bliss, happiness, recognition, union: love.

DAPHNE ROSE KINGMA
author of True Love *and* Heart & Soul

Romantic Anticipations

"The erotic is not a question only of what we do; it is a question of how acutely and fully we can feel in the doing."

AUDRE LORDE

*H*e is a god in my eyes—
the man who is allowed to sit beside you—he

who listens intimately
to the sweet murmur of
your voice, the enticing

laughter that makes my own
heart beat fast. If I meet
you suddenly, I can't

speak—my tongue is broken;
a thin flame runs under
my skin; seeing nothing,
hearing only my own ears
drumming, I drip with sweat;
trembling shakes my body

and I turn paler than
dry grass. At such times
death isn't far from me

SAPPHO

$\mathcal{K}$indle, in the hearth, the last fire of the year! The sun and the flame together will illuminate your face.

O last fire of the year! The last, the most lovely! Your peony pink, disheveled, fills the hearth with an endlessly blossoming shower of sparks. Let us lean toward it, offer it our hands, which its glow penetrates and bloodies. There is not one flower in our garden more beautiful than it, a tree more complicated, a grass more full of motion, a creeper so treacherous, so imperious! Let us stay here, let us cherish this changing god who makes a smile dance in your melancholy eyes . . .

Later on, when I take off my dress, you will see me all pink like a painted statue. I will stand motionless before it, and in the panting glow my skin will seem to quicken, to tremble and move as in the hours when love, with an inevitable wing, swoops down on me . . . Let's stay! The last fire of the year invites us to silence, idleness, and tender repose. With my head on your breast, I can hear the wind, the flames, and your heart all beating, while at the black windowpane a branch of the pink peach tree taps incessantly, half unleaved, terrified, and undone like a bird in a storm . . .

COLETTE
"The Last Fire"

The clear bead at the center changes everything.
There are no edges to my loving now.

I've heard it said there's a window that opens
from one mind to another,

but if there's no wall, there's no need
for fitting the window, or the latch.

RUMI

~

Taking the hands of someone you love,
You see they are delicate cages...
Tiny birds are singing
In the secluded prairies
And in the deep valleys of the hands.

ROBERT BLY
"Taking the Hands"

9

$\mathscr{L}$et me dwell in the light of thine eyes,
Let me find a sweet home in thy heart!
For my soul like a wild bird flies,
To linger wherever thou art—
As night give place to the day,
And darkness before the sun flies,
So my sorrows will all melt away,
When I live in the light of thine eyes.

VICTORIAN VERSE

~

$\mathscr{W}$e embraced each other with—how to say it—a momentous calm, as if the cup of language had silently overflowed into these eloquent kisses which replaced words like the rewards of silence itself, perfecting thought and gesture.

LAWRENCE DURRELL

$\mathscr{M}$aking love is more than simple physical self-indulgence, biological release. It is a dialogue between two souls, the interface of the material and spiritual.

If you are disappointed in your sexual relationship, ask yourself how your view of sex may have limited the quality of your intimate experience. And the next time you make love, allow yourself to partake of it not just as a physical pleasure but an encounter with the holy.

DAPHNE ROSE KINGMA

~

$\mathscr{I}$will make you brooches and toys for
        your delight
Of birdsong at morning and starshine at
        night.

ROBERT LOUIS STEVENSON

*S*ex is saved from self-destruction by eros, and this is the normal condition. But eros cannot live without *philia*, brotherly love and friendship. The tension of continuous attraction and continuous passion would be unbearable if it lasted forever. *Philia* is the relaxation in the presence of the beloved which accepts the other's being; it is simply liking to be with the other, liking to rest with the other, liking the rhythm of the walk, the voice, the whole being of the other. This gives a width to eros; it gives it time to grow; time to sink its roots down deeper. *Philia* does not require that we do anything for the beloved except accept him, be with him, and enjoy him. It is friendship in the simplest, most direct terms.

ROLLO MAY

*G*o deeper than love, for the goal has greater depths,
love is like the grass, but the heart is deep wild rock
molten, yet dense and permanent.

Go down to your old deep heart, and lose sight of
       yourself.
And lose sight of me, the me whom you turbulently
       loved.

Let us lose sight of ourselves, and break the mirrors.
For the fierce curve of our lives is moving again to
       the depths
out of sight, in the deep living heart.

          D. H. LAWRENCE
          from "*Know Deeply, Know Thyself*
          More Deeply"

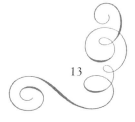

$\mathscr{L}$awrence Durrell wrote in *Clea*, "I am hunting for metaphors which might convey something of the piercing happiness too seldom granted to those who love; but words, which were first invented against despair, are too crude to mirror the properties of something so profoundly at peace with itself. Words are the mirrors of our discontents merely: they contain all the unhatched eggs of the world's sorrows."

Words do make the mood. We all know the usual terms of endearment—*honey, dear, sweetie, angel,* to name just a few. But to fan the flames of passion and romance, why not try some less tired language, like *sweeting, sweetling,* or *sweetikin* (in vogue the sixteenth and seventeenth centuries). Or how about *dearling* (the original form of *darling*). Your partner could become your *paramour* (literally, *through love* in French). Instead of *attractive* or *cute,* try *toothsome* or *cuddlesome*. Rather than *missing,* try *yearning, pining, longing,* or *hungering* and see the ardor build.

$\mathscr{I}$unpetalled you, like a rose,
to see your soul,
and I didn't see it.

But everything around
—horizons of lands and of seas—
everything, out to the infinite,
was filled with a fragrance,
enormous and alive.

> JUAN RAMON JIMENEZ
> translated by Stephen Mitchell

~

$\mathscr{C}$ome, let us make love deathless, thou and I.

> HERBERT TRENCH

The scent of rain on warm earth reminds
me darling of your sweet breath. And those small
    winds that
uncurl the deodar flowers petal by petal
and drenched in that heady sap blow south,
I grasp, embrace, pretending it's you.
But darling, my excuse,
if any ask why I'm making a fool of myself
making love to thin air,
is that no breeze could be so fragrant
had it not first caressed your body.

KALIDASA
from *The Cloud Messenger*

O my body! I dare not desert the likes of you in other
    men and women, nor the likes of the parts of you,
I believe the likes of you are to stand or fall with the
    likes of the soul,
(and that they are the soul,)
I believe the likes of you shall stand or fall with my
    poems, and that they are my poems,
Man's, woman's, child's youth's wife's husband's,
    mother's, father's, young man's young woman's
    poems,
Head, neck, hair, ears, drop and tympan of the ears,
Eyes, eye-fringes, iris of the eye, eyebrows, and the
    waking or
sleeping of the lids,
Mouth, tongue, lips, teeth, roof of the mouth, jaws, and
    the jaw-hinges,
Nose, nostrils of the nose, and the partition,
Cheeks, temples, forehead, chin, throat, back of the
    neck, neck-slue,
Strong shoulders, manly beard, scapula, hind-shoulders,
    and the
ample side-round of the chest,
Upper-arm, armpit, elbow-socket, lower-arm, arm-
    sinews, arm-bones,

Wrist and wrist-joints, hand, palm, knuckles, thumb,
    forefinger,
finger-joints, finger-nails,
Broad breast-front, curling hair of the breast, breast-
    bone, breast-side,
Ribs, belly, backbone, joints of the backbone,
Hips, hip-sockets, hip-strength, inward and outward
    round, man-balls, man-root,
Strong set of thighs, well carrying the trunk above,
Leg-fibres, knee, knee-pan, upper-leg, under-leg,
Ankles, instep, foot-ball, toes, toe-joints, the heel;
All attitudes, all the shapeliness, all the belongings of
    my or your body of any one's body, male or female,
The lung-sponges, the stomach-sac, the bowels sweet
    and clean,
The brain in its folds inside the skull-frame,
Sympathies, heart-valves, palate-valves, sexuality, mater-
    nity,
Womanhood and all that is a woman, and the man that
    comes from
woman,
The womb, the teats, nipples breast-milk, tears, laughter,
    weeping,
    love-looks, love-perturbations and risings,
    The voice, articulation, language, whispering, shouting
aloud,

Food, drink, pulse, digestion, sweat, sleep, walking, swimming,

Poise on the hips, leaping, reclining, embracing, arm-curving and

tightening,

The continual changes of the flex of the mouth, and around the eyes,

The skin, the sunburnt shade, freckles, hair,

The curious sympathy one feels when feeling with the hand the

naked meat of the body,

The circling rivers the breath, and breathing it in and out,

The beauty of the waist, and thence of the hips, and thence down-ward toward the knees,

The thin red jellies within you or within me, the bones and the

marrow in the bones,

The exquisite realization of health;

O say these are not the parts and poems of the body only, but of

the

soul,

O say now these are the soul!

WALT WHITMAN

19

Walking into the dawn, the dawn was apple-green
while I felt the gentle rain on my eyelashes,
my cheeks, my tongue
and underneath the soles of my feet the moist earth,
the puddles in between wet soil, bedewed grass,
and I keep walking into the dawn,
into the rain so generous with its caress,
the dawn was apple-green,
and all around me the orchard of desire,
the trees swollen with fruit
waiting for the loving touch of the migratory picker,
the dawn was apple-green, and I was stalking the ripe,
the damask daystar, the beginning of joy
walking into the dawn, into the orchard of desire,
before me, behind me, surrounding my timid flesh,
trees swollen with ripe fruit,
and underneath their flowering branches
bushels like empty bottles praying for the claret,
the peach wine, rose wine, cherry wine,
wine-red, wine-colored, blood-red apples,
peaches, berries, pears, yellow pears smooth as silk,
and the dawn was apple-green, walking into the dawn,
the dawn was apple-green when I first met you . . .

ROCHELLE   LYNN HOLT
"Yellow Pears, Smooth as Silk"

You are what sculptors search for in stone,
the summer and sun I have been struggling toward,
surrender that comes hard,
gaiety I had thought gone, more.
The restless touch of your hand,
like relentless waves reaching for blond sand,
and delivering small dead fish to shore.
I remember the need I created you with,
the dream I summoned you from,
that desire placed a trench in the floor of my mind
worrying you wouldn't come.
Your thrilling touch is a sieve
that separates my willing body from impeding
        thought,
that handles me like a moan.
Woman, I loved you before you were grown,
and reached for you when you were foam
left in a beer mug, settling into lonely beach sand,
        an ache.
Dear, I will surprise you with devotion as strong
as the hurt in your eyes,
as deep as the scars in Jesus' palms

        FRANK LAMONT PHILLIPS
        "Love Poem"

21

$\mathcal{R}$omance is the champagne and frosted glasses of love, the magic that gives love a tango to dance to, a fragrance to remember, and a fantasy-come-true to hold in your heart. Romance is the antidote to ordinariness, the inspiration for passion; whenever you fold it into your relationship, you instantly elevate it to a more delicious state of being. Romanced, you feel beautiful or handsome; life becomes ripe with hope; the moon, stars, and planets bathe you in a cascade of beneficent light; and you believe everything is possible—your sweetest, wildest, and most cherished dreams will certainly come true.

At least that's certainly how we feel in the rosy blush of new romance. But the feeling of romance doesn't just stick around all by itself. As time goes on, it takes effort, ingenuity, intuition, and sometimes even a willingness to feel foolish, to keep the moonlight magical. That's because somewhere along the line, without quite paying attention, we stop doing the things that kindled romance in the first place: we forget to bring the long-stemmed roses and to whisper sweet nothings; we leave the lights on (or off); we trade in the black lingerie for flannel pajamas. In short, we start treating one another as roommates instead of passionate lovers.

But we can still have romance in our lives, no matter how long we've been together. Chill the glasses. Remember the roses. Install the new dimmer, light the candles and forget about the wax dripping on the table, play the song you first heard on your honeymoon. Dress the bed in red sheets. Drive up the hill to watch the sunset and kiss (and kiss) in the car. Don't let opportunities slip through the cracks.

DAPHNE ROSE KINGMA

~

All great lovers are articulate, and verbal seduction is the surest road to actual seduction.

MARYA MANNES

My heart will always fly to you like a bird, from any place on earth, and it will surely find you . . . that you had become so much a part of the Heaven that stretches above me that I had only to raise up my eyes to be by your side. And even if they flung me into a dungeon, that piece of Heaven would still spread out within me and my heart would fly up to it like a bird, and that is why everything is so simple, so terribly simple and beautiful and full of meaning.

ETTY HILLESUM

~

But this dark is deep:
now I warm you with my blood, listen
to this flesh.
It is far truer than poems.

MARINA TSVETAYEVA

If only you would touch my heart,
if only you would put your lips to my heart,
your delicate mouth, your teeth,
if you would place your tongue like a red arrow
where my crumbling heart is beating,
if you would blow over my heart, near the sea, crying,
it would ring with an obscure sound, the sound of train
wheels,
of dreams,
like the to and fro of waters,
like autumn in leaf,
like blood,
with a noise of damp flames burning the sky,
dreaming like dreams, or branches, or winds,
or the horns of some sad port,
if you would blow on my heart near the sea
like a white ghost would blow,
on the lace of the spume,
in the cut of the wind,
like an unchained ghost crying at the sea's edge.

PABLO NERUDA
from *Barcarole*

On a Tuesday during a waxing moon,
in the fifth hour after sunset:

Light a red candle.
Place a glass of water next to the candle.
Place before the candle, in a natural vessel:
lavender
rosemary
violet
cinnamon
Dab the candle with vanilla and musk.

Focus your attention on your heart center.
Imagine energy drawing up through your body from
the earth
and emanating from your heart center.

SAY ALOUD:
   Our fire is passion, our water is lust,
   The earth of our bodies melts in the air of our
       desires.

With the blessing of the Universe
I ask that infinite passions between us ignite.
So be it.
And so it is.

Blow out the candle, but save it for use in a romantic moment.
Drink the water.

Place the herbs discretely in your bedroom.

> BARRIE DOLNICK
> *Primary Spell for Reigning Passion*

In the spring twilight

The full moon is shining:
Girls take their places as though around an altar

And their feet move

Rhythmically, as tender
feet of Cretan girls
dance once around an

altar of love, crushing
a circle in the soft
smooth flowering grass

Awed by her splendor

Stars near the lovely
moon cover their own
bright faces
when she
is roundest and lights
earth with her silver

Now, while we dance

Come here to us
gentle Gaiety,
Revelry, Radiance

and you, Muses
with lovely hair

SAPPHO

My peace is gone
My heart is sore
I'll find it never
Never more.

My breast desires
And longs for him
Could I but hold
And cling to him

And kiss him as
I long to kiss
And with his kisses
Die of bliss.

JOHANN WOLFGANG VON GOETHE
from *Faust*

*I*n China, intercourse is seen as the fusion of *K'an* and *Li.*

K'an is female, the moon and water. Li is the male, sun and fire. That's a beautiful way to think of the common difference in sexual readiness between men and women, one that perhaps can diffuse conflict a couple may have over timing.

~

I am yours forever
And our co-equal love
will make the stars
to laugh with joy.

CHRISTINA WALSH

31

Give all to love;
Obey thy heart,
Friends, kindred, days,
Estate, good fame,
plans, credit, and the Muse—
Nothing refuse.

'Tis a brave master;
Let it have scope:
Follow it utterly,
Hope beyond hope:
High and more high
It dives into noon,
With wing unspent,
Untold intent;
But it is a god,
Knows its own path,
And the outlets of the sky.

It was never for the mean;
It requireth courage stout,
Souls above doubt,
Valour unbending:
Such 'twill reward;—
They shall return
More than they were,
And ever ascending.

RALPH WALDO EMERSON
"Give All to Love"

*W*ater (woman) that is the essence of you.
He na tye (woman) that is recognition and remembering.
Gentle. Soft. Sure.
Long shadows of afternoon, growing as the light turns
west toward sleep. Turning with the sun.
(The rest of it is continents and millennia.
(How could I have waited so long for completion?)

The water rises around us like the goddess coming
home.
(Arisen.) Same trip, all things considered, all times
and visions, all places and spaces taken into account
on that ancient journey, finally returned. The maps,
the plans,
the timetables: the carefully guided tours into all
manner
of futilities. Manners the last turn in the road: arid
irony.

(Lady, why does your love so touch me?
(Lady, why do my hands have strength for you?
(Lady, how could I have wandered so long without
you?

> PAULA   GUNN ALLEN
> from "He Na Tye Woman"

You can learn to enjoy your sensuality in each and every moment. Right now, listening to music, let the music vibrate the pores of your skin. Washing dishes, let the suds bathe your hands. Walking the dog, learn to enjoy being pulled. Every day there are hundreds of things you can enjoy. You can enjoy the leisureliness of a stroll, or the sweat of jogging, or the tang of a breeze. Every moment can be an experience that lets you grow in sensuality. Right now you can feel this paper, this book, this space, the sounds around you, even your own breathing. Being open to all that and with all that will gradually turn you on to life more and more.

WILLIAM ASHOKA ROSS

$\mathcal{I}$walk out, blindly.
The stars have fallen,
the night is sharp black obsidian, cutting.
Stars are encrusted on the ground
around roots, and flower stems
crunch under feet.
My skin is wind-pricked

In spite of myself I seem to be alive.

This life, splendid and terrible,
ambushes me from the thicket.
It is always that way.
And all the love and fear of me
tucked within you
or spilling from you,
and all that is remembered
or forgotten of us,

and all that yet crouches in the thicket
that is fierce and benevolent both,
and all the love
and all the fury,
and all the succulence and foolishness,
the truth and the ruthlessness,
what is within us and between us
and planted by each in the pith of us,
will overtake us and stun us
some day or night
no less beautiful than this.

> MICHAEL HILL
> "I walk out, blindly"

37

I

Love me, sweet, with all thou art,
  Feeling, thinking, seeing, —
Love me in the lightest part,
  Love me in full being.

II

Love me with thine open youth
  In its frank surrender;
With thy vowing of thy mouth,
  With its silence tender.

III

Love me with thine azure eyes,
  Made for earnest granting!
Taking colour from the skies,
  Can Heaven's truth be wanting?

IV

Love me with their lids, that fall
  Snow-like at first meeting;
Love me with thine heart, that all
  The neighbours then see beating.

V

Love me with thine hand stretched out
  Freely--open-minded;
Love me with thy loitering foot, —
  Hearing one behind it.

VI

Love me with thy voice, that turns
  Sudden faint above me;
Love me with thy blush that burns
  When I murmur, *Love me!*

ELIZABETH BARRETT BROWNING
"A Man's Requirements"

39

$\mathcal{W}$hat's in a word? Shakespeare did say that "a rose by any other name would smell as sweet," but is that true for our language for sexual organs? So much of the sexual terminology in English is crude, shame-based, or scientific. In many Eastern countries, on the other hand, sexual language is much more poetic and romantic, exhibiting a genuine delight with pleasure.

For example, *inner heart* is one of the ancient Chinese terms for vagina, whereas a penis was often referred to as a *jade scepter*. They called vaginal secretions *the dew of ecstasy*. An orgasm was referred to as *clouds and rain* (*clouds* refers to female love juices; *rain* to semen). China was not the only place with such terms. Sanskrit words for the sexual organs stem from a cultural background in which women were honored as embodiments of divine female energy, and genitals were seen as sacred symbols of the god and goddess.

Here's some other language you might like to try out:

Vagina

> *jade gate:* TAOIST
> *golden gate:* CHINESE
> *doorway of life:* CHINESE
> *mysterious valley:* CHINESE
> *pillow of music:* CHINESE
> *yoni:* SANSKRIT, also means *origin* or *source*
> *lotus:* CHINESE
> *the delicious:* TURKISH

Penis

> *lingum:* SANSKRIT; also is the image of the god
> > Shiva
> *ambassador:* CHINESE
> *jade flute:* CHINESE
> *jade peak:* CHINESE
> *crimson bird:* CHINESE
> *arrow of love:* TANTRIC
> *diamond scepter:* SANSKRIT

41

*L*ying asleep between the strokes of night
    I saw my love lean over my sad bed,
    Pale as the duskiest lily's leaf or head,
Smooth-skinned and dark, with bare throat made to
    bite,
Too wan for blushing and too warm for white,
    But perfect-coloured without white or red.
    And her lips opened amorously, and said—
I wish not what, saving one word—Delight.
And all her face was honey to my mouth,
    And all her body pasture to mine eyes;
    The long lithe arms and hotter hands than fire,
The quivering flanks, hair smelling of the south,
The bright light feet, the splendid supple thighs
    And glittering eyelids of my soul's desire.

        ALGERNON CHARLES SWINBURNE
        "Love and Sleep"

When we were born, we were torn from wholeness; in love we have all felt ourselves returning to the original wholeness. That is why poetic images transform the beloved into nature—a mountain, water, a cloud, a star, a wood, the sea, a wave—and why in turn nature speaks to us as though it were a lover. Reconciliation with the totality of the world. With past, present, and future as well. Love is not eternity; nor it is the time of calendars and watches, successive time. The time of love is neither great nor small; it is the perception of all times, of all lives, in a single instant. . . . What does the couple see in the space of an instant, a blink of an eye? The equation of appearance and disappearance, the truth of the body and the nonbody, the vision of the presence that dissolves into splendor: pure vitality, a heartbeat of time.

OCTAVIO PAZ

$\mathcal{W}$hen it comes to kindling romance, you have to be willing to be creative, even if at first you feel shy or embarrassed. Remember, you weren't embarrassed by all those love notes and love songs when you were falling in love. The art of romance takes practice. The more you allow yourself to stretch the limits of what feels comfortable to you, the more inventive you'll become, especially if your initial efforts garner a positive response. (And if you're the receiver of these endeavors to enchant, be sure to respond. If you do, you'll increase the romance quotient in your life.)

Whatever your particular romantic preferences may be, be sure to indulge them as much as you can. Like the love it will embellish, romance is a very special art form whose reward is the joy of passion.

DAPHNE ROSE KINGMA

and when his good love is done
a man is a low-down, a troublesome thing
he'll leave you to sing

*S*he hates to see that western sun go down. Summer's heat mingles with desire / a sullen sweat that clings—a glistening second umber skin. It's too tight. It's too hot. She feels that primal yearn.

Whooowheee.

She aches for seduction / his lips pressing in on hers. She aches to yield to his manful grasp working her back, her shoulders, her breasts. She can almost inhale that pungent musk opening her nose, obliterating all thought. She can almost feel the touch of him—skin-to-skin / more than naked, the total loss of self as she submits / becomes a mass of sensation freed of the world and its psychotic quest for the new and orderly.

She suffers a euphoric vision: she and he embraced / one, a precise orchestration of hands and tongues amove in fevered rhythm / writhings in that sacred expanse / possessed. He and she arching, reaching through one another—he and she beyond exaltation—*there*. And the trumpets sound and the walls yield.

Decrescendo—a honeyed sopping slide down . . . down . . . Surrendered.

Oh—to once more smell that fish-stink after sex. The holy odor of gorged lust.

The children sleep unmindful of Mama's tortured restlessness. At times they've seen her bemoaning that past. At times they've seen her bemoaning their uncertain present. Now they awaken and surprise her, stumbling from the dark to suddenly quell those moans and sobs. And in their hapless / helpless concern comes the confused and loving whine of *Mama what's wrong*. She answers through tears and shudders. *Mama is sad is all. Don't be worried. Everything will be all right.* She hugs them and kisses them and sends them back to their dreams.

What could she tell them? She didn't know their marriage wouldn't last. She didn't know the kind of man he'd become. She didn't know she'd grow apart and part from him finally. And she didn't know the price she'd have to pay and keep paying. She didn't know, then, what would be demanded in sacrifice—or what it would extract in exquisite anguish. She had no idea of the limits of her fortitude or the strength of her weaknesses. But now she's growing aware—beginning to discover the fierce gluttony of flesh freed of matrimony:

That complexity of blood, bone, gristle, muscle and fat . . . that fiery vessel of steamy rut. That awareness that exudes sensuality and sex merely by being— effortlessly. And when she adds her mind to it, when love comes down on her, that's the worst time. That explicit urge overtakes / damns her.

She sits quietly on the floor by the stereo. She goes through her record collection, a stroll down memory lane. She needs some of that soothe for the beastly savage a prowl in her veins tonight. Something to lull / temper / arrest it. A ritual dance through lost loves. Recollected moments—the cherished and the shameful. The first dance at a sock hop. The first house party. Prom night and the hymen breaking. The night he and she merged and conceived. Any memory to cling to, to keep her anchored and sane. Anything to relieve her of this raving heat. Anything to retrieve equanimity.

She searches for the proper sound, the one to counteract this particular mood—perhaps exorcise it. And she decides on the 45s. Some raw funk: Bobby Blue Bland goin' down slow, Syl Johnson only havin' love to give, the stomp down bump and grind of Mama's baby Daddy's maybe Swamp Dogg, James Brown grieving oh Mary don't you weep, Al Green in love and happiness, the Impressions inviting love to paradise,

'Spoon spewing bad bad whiskey losin' him a happy home, Otis Redding making admonitions about Cupid (he's not stupid), or the wicked Mr. Pickett's Mustang Sally refusing to slow her Mustang down.

She rises. She lets the music possess her and she cuts free, going for all she knows. Her head is soaked and her hair goes all the way back to Africa. She bends, turns, spins until she's one with that sound. One pulse. One throb hip-quaking—a frenzy working her way through steps she knows as intimately as the scars on her psyche; the shimmy, the hully-gully, the stroll, the skate, the four corners, the sophisticated sissy, the fat man, the charge, the bugaloo, the break down. She walks a dog and she shakes her tail feather. She mother pops corn in bare feet. The sound consumes her and she speaks in tongues.

Collapsed to the floor, she lies there for how long? Until summoned by the scratch of the needle's bounce at the end of a track, as the automatic return fails to re-activate. She can barely hear it above her heart still dancing inside her. And she groans. She groans. She wails. She chants *have mercy have mercy on me*. The hurt remains. And it is grown deeper than before. Down to her soul's bone.

She draws her bath. She's so hot the warm water begins to sizzle and bubble as she sinks into the tub.

She bathes thoroughly but hastily. She can no longer wait. Her mind fixed on what she's driven to enact. She dries off quickly and liberally applies creams and potions to dispel ashiness, satisfied as her umber skin takes on satiny luster. She oils, braids and blow-dries her hair. It takes twenty minutes but the result is an ebony bush of silk. And now the smoky knit hose. And now the black strapless bra. And now the ebony mini-slip. And now an abbreviated top layer of gold lamé. She slips on black patent leather pumps. And her purse. What does she need? Her driver's license, her little money—enough for two drinks. It seldom takes long before some mother's son is paying her tab. The keys, her 'fro pick, a few tissues in the tiny shoulder bag. She won't have to ask anyone to watch her purse, it'll go right nicely with her on the dance floor.

In the mirror she feels beautiful—radiant—as she anoints herself in sterling silver and 14 carat gold.

She checks the windows. She checks the back door. She turns on the radio to ward off potential intruders. She'll leave the light on in the bathroom. She'll leave the television on as well. She'll leave a note taped to the telephone—in case. . . .She tiptoes to the children's room and looks in on them. She closes her eyes and envisions a white light around them. She opens her eyes and takes in their gentle breathing. She whispers, *Mama loves you.* She checks for and notes the pink glow of the night light protecting against an all consuming dark. She blows them a kiss and quietly closes the door.

It's so close—that midnight hour.

She secures the door behind her and high steps into the ultramarine cool of ghetto night as it licks her thighs. A jolt of expectation shoots through her as she hastens along that familiar avenue certain of her destination / that honky tonk haven, that urbane piety of flesh hunters and soulful survivors. She knows he's there waiting. She knows his voraciousness is mate to her own. She knows he is a lover of music and madnesses—a man given birth by an upright piano, a guitar, a trombone, a set of skins and *beat me Daddy eight to the bar.*

She knows what his Mama done taught him. And she knows he no longer bothers with or cares what Mama said.

And her walk becomes a strut with a swing and a dip to her arrogant hip asway to the throb of traffic—to the staccato of her heels against that eternal pavement going clickitty-clack clickitty-clack echoing back . . .

> WANDA COLEMAN
> "The Blues in the Night"

Ardent Advances

"*The kiss is the gateway to bliss.*"
<small>KAMA SUTRA</small>

The erotic instinct...belongs, on the one hand, to the original animal nature of man, which will exist as long as man has an animal body. On the other hand, it is connected with the highest forms of the spirit. But it blooms only when spirit and instinct are in true harmony. If one or the other aspect is missing, then an injury occurs, or at least there is a one-sided lack of balance which easily slips into the pathological. Too much of the animal disfigures the civilized human being, too much culture makes a sick animal.

CARL JUNG

~

A thousand kisses grant me sweet;
With a hundred these complete;
Lip me a thousand more, and then
Another hundred give again.
A thousand more, then hurry one
Kiss after kiss without cessation
Until we lose all calculation . . .

CATULLUS

A relationship needs to be S.W.A.K. Remember that? It meant that the letter you sent, the words you wrote, and the feelings you had were made more dear because you sealed them with a kiss.

Even when the courtship is over, the love you live needs to be sealed and affirmed again and again with a multitude of kisses. For kisses, the loving embrace of the lips, are the sign, more than almost anything else, that we like, love, cherish, and adore the person we are kissing.

Kisses, like those little candy hearts on Valentine's Day, can carry all our little (and big and magnificent) messages of love. They are the sweetest, simplest, common denominator expression of love. Whenever we give them to one another we are nurturing our bond.

As kisses are the portal to erotic life in new romance, so they are the life support system of erotic passion in a longtime love. They are the emblem of passionate contact, the way we tell one another that we love and that we would like to make love.

But kisses aren't simply the key-card to erotic passion, and, once having entered the realm of sexual intimacy, we need to remember that kisses also have a power and a beauty of their own. Kisses can and should have a multitude of meanings. They can be the sign that true love is about to begin, they can be the communication of affection, they can be the counterpoint to passion. Wordless, they speak everything from "Honey, I'm home," to "Congratulations"; "I'm wild about you"; "Darling, I adore you"; "You're the one I desire"; "I'm yours"; to "I'm sorry." But whatever their specific function at the moment, kisses say we want to be attached to, come home to, and spiritually embrace the person we are kissing.

Kisses are the food of love. They make us feel . . . kissed. Chosen, desirable, powerful, beautiful, sensual, joyful, happy, carefree, invincible, LOVED. Kisses lift the level of our experience from daily and banal to delicious and extraordinary. Kisses capture our attention, and express our best intentions. So shower each other with kisses and never underestimate the power of a kiss.

DAPHNE ROSE KINGMA

$\mathcal{W}$ithout warning

As a whirlwind
swoops on an oak
Love shakes my heart

If you will come

I shall put out
new pillows for
you to rest on

Thank you, my dear

You came, and you did
well to come: I needed
you. You have made

love blaze up in
my breasts—bless you!
Bless you as often

as the hours have
been endless to me
while you were gone

I was so happy

Believe me, I
prayed that that
night might be
doubled for us

Now I know why Eros,

Of all the progeny of
Earth and Heaven, has
been most dearly loved

SAPPHO

Clouds out of darkness,
Pillow white, they float,
As dawn slides open.
Slowly, the kinswoman
Parachutes gentle free
Arriving with gravity,
Cleaving, to earth,
As Seagull does to nest.

Oracle of all dreams,
Chalice, shelter, wing,
Harvesting molten treasure,
Flowing through sun gold
Feathers and life air
        of Anatolia.

Ancient fire haired druid,
            mariner,
Tiamat, Diana, moon world
            goddess,

Eating the ripe sea,
      the sensuous air,
Gleaning and swelling
      the life source
Into a vivid, retina burning,
      sun flood.
Drenching all completeness
      with desire
To search sweet for
      inner seed,
Kindling, bringing to light
      what is
Herself, the kinswoman.

SUZANNE BENTON
"The Second Coming"

With a chaste heart,
with pure eyes,
I celebrate your beauty
holding the leash of blood
so that it might leap out
and trace your outline
where
you lie down in my ode
as in a land of forests, or in surf:
in aromatic loam
or in sea-music.

Beautiful nude:
equally beautiful
your feet
arched by primeval tap
of wind or sound;
your ears
small shells
of the splendid American sea;
your breasts
of level plentitude full-
filled by living light;

your flying
eyelids of wheat
revealing
or enclosing
the two deep countries of your eyes.

The line your shoulders
have divided
into pale regions
loses itself and blends
into the compact halves
of an apple,
continues separating
your beauty down
into two columns
of burnished gold, fine alabaster,
to sink into the two grapes of your feet,
where your twin symmetrical tree
burns again and rises:
flowering fire, open chandelier,
a swelling fruit
over the pact of sea and earth.

From what materials—
agate, quartz, wheat—
did your body come together,
swelling like baking bread
to signal silvered
hills,
the cleavage of one petal,
sweet fruits of a deep velvet,
until alone remained,
astonished,
the fine and firm feminine form?

It is not only light that falls
over the world,
spreading inside your body
its suffocated snow,
so much as clarity
taking its leave of you
as if you were
on fire within.

The moon lives in the lining of your skin.

PABLO NERUDA
"Ode to a Beautiful Nude"

$\mathscr{I}$t's worth your while, if you want great sex, to create a bedroom that's ideally conducive to intimacy. It doesn't need to be expensively furnished, but it should be clean and uncluttered, have pleasing colors, and not be merely utilitarian; it should inspire a sense of beauty. The bed you use for sex ought to have a special, exotic, other-worldly feeling, almost evocative of an altar. There should be an air of reverence. Some people enjoy making love under a canopy, and you may want to construct one. Soft lighting is immensely helpful, and so is quietly pulsating music. When the whole room feels like a retreat from the hustle and bustle of everyday life, won't you relish the thought of spending time there with your beloved?

WILLIAM ASHOKA ROSS

This is the female form,
A divine nimbus exhales from it from head to foot,
It attracts with fierce undeniable attraction,
I am drawn by its breath as if I were no more than a
    helpless vapor,
all falls aside but myself and it,
Books, art, religion, time, the visible and solid earth,
    and what was expected of heaven or fear'd of hell,
    are now consumed,
Mad filaments, ungovernable shoots play out of it, the
    response
likewise ungovernable,
Hair, bosom, hips, bend of legs, negligent falling hands
    all diffused,
mine too diffused,

Ebb stung by the flow and flow stung by the ebb, love-
    flesh swelling
and deliciously aching,
Limitless limpid jets of love hot and enormous, quiver-
    ing jelly of
love, white-blow and delirious juice,
Bridegroom night of love working surely and softly into
    the prostrate
dawn,
Undulating into the willing and yielding day,
Lost in the cleave of the clasping and sweet-flesh'd day.

WALT WHITMAN

And when he arrived home, there was no sign between them. He waited and waited till she came. And as he waited, his limbs seemed strong and splendid to him, his hands seemed like passionate servants to him, goodly, he felt a stupendous power in himself, of life, and of urgent, strong blood.

She was sure to come at last, and touch him. Then he burst into flame for her, and lost himself. They looked at each other, a deep laugh at the bottom of their eyes, and he went to take of her again, wholesale, mad to revel in the inexhaustible wealth of her, to bury himself in the depths of her in an inexhaustible exploration, she all the while revelling in that he revelled in her, tossed all her secrets aside and plunged to that which was secret to her as well, whilst she quivered with fear and the last anguish of delight.

> D. H. LAWRENCE
> from *The Rainbow*

Aphrodisiacs, named for Aphrodite, the goddess of love, are edible substances said to enhance physical passion. Throughout history, a multitude of substances have been believed to be effective in enhancing ardor; seafood, especially oysters and caviar, tops many lists. "According to the Greek poet Aschepiades," notes *The Encyclopedia of Erotic Wisdom*, "it was customary to take along twenty-four prawns plus three large and ten small fish when going to visit a courtesan."

Other "love potions" include garlic, truffles, cinnamon, honey, chocolate, ginseng, pumpkin, bee pollen, and eggs. On the more esoteric list are brains, camel fat and milk, rhino horn, Spanish fly, menstrual blood, sweat, saliva, and semen.

THE KISSING GAME

A game is established

> Only kisses on the mouth are intended, not any-
> where else. Passion is stirred up by a kissing compe-
> tition. It is a game, since there is a winner and a
> loser.

> The first to seize the other's lip is the winner. As in
> a game, it is necessary to take the other by surprise.
> Since there is a winner, a quarrel is inevitable,
> which is also a stimulant. If she loses, she cries a
> little and wrings her hands, she sighs, threatens
> him, bites him and then, turning round, she draws
> him to her forcefully, ill-treats and insults him. If he
> wins again, she ill-treats him doubly.

The trick (kapatadyuta)

Taking advantage of the self-satisfied hero's
inattention, the heroine catches his lip with her
teeth and immobilizes him. If he protests, she
threatens him, shakes him, dances about joyfully
waving her arms and telling him some home
truths.

She loudly boasts of her victory. If her lover gets
cross, she challenges him, her eyes dancing and
arms waving until he shows his strength. Thus
finishes the affectionate conflict of the war of kisses.

KAMA SUTRA

$\mathcal{E}$xperiment sexually. . . . It probably doesn't work to have a script, but having talked about your sexual feelings or proclivities, you and your partner should have a sense of where you want to go. If the two of you are always in the same position, you might want to vary it. If the course of your lovemaking follows a predictable pattern, you might want to talk about ways of creating a different sequence of events. This might be something as basic as who initiates and who responds. Try doing it the other way. And if your initiation is verbal, try something physical. If lovemaking usually begins with someone's hand reaching out, try a well-placed whisper in your partner's ear, inviting him to do something that is not discussed in polite company.

ALAN EPSTEIN

The triangle of a man's shoulders, back, and hips, moving as he moves, gliding, turning. The delicate hollow at the base of a woman's neck, that pulsating depression, that gentle U of bone, the plain of soft skin below. And the fetish goes on, enlarging, clarifying. A falling corner of clothing, the slither of sheets. Acts are like this, too, so fraught with erotic potential, they take on the characteristics of objects: to *do* a certain thing, to slip a hand between the buttons on a lover's shirt. The act is infinitely variable, infinitely repeatable, the way an object is always new and always there.

SALLIE TISDALE
from *Talk Dirty to Me*

The moth's kiss, first!
Kiss me as if you made believe
You were not sure, this eve,
How my face, your flower, had pursed
Its petals up; so, here and there
You brush it, till I grow aware
Who wants me, and wide open I burst.

ROBERT BROWNING
from "In a Gondola"

~

Her breath is like honey spiced with cloves,
Her mouth delicious as a ripened mango.
To press kisses on her skin is to taste the lotus,
The deep cave of her navel hides a store of spices
What pleasure lies beyond, the tongue knows,
But cannot speak of it.

SRNGARAKARIKA
Kumaradatta

*H*as your kissing gotten boring? It doesn't have to be. The *Kama Sutra* and *Tibetan Arts of Love* describe five modalities of kissing: lipping, sucking, biting, tonguing, and blowing, each of which can be done at pressures from hard to soft, speeds from fast to slow, and at various depths from shallow to deep. You can also kiss upper and lower lips separately and together, kiss both inner and outer lip and trade kissing and being kissed. Combined, there are literally hundreds of variations. Give them *all* a try.

Dissolver of sugar, dissolve me,
if this is the time.
Do it gently with a touch of a hand, or a look.
Every morning I wait at
dawn. That's when it's happened before.
Or do it suddenly like an execution. How else can I
get ready for death?

You breathe without a body like a spark.
You grieve, and I begin to feel lighter.
You keep me away with your arm,
but the keeping away is pulling me in.

> RUMI
> "Dissolver of Sugar"

At the last, tenderly,
From the walls of the powerful fortress'd house,
From the clasp of the knitted locks, from the keep of
    the well-closed doors,
Let me be wafted.
Let me glide noiselessly forth;
With the key of softness unlock the locks—with a
    whisper,
Set open the doors O soul.
Tenderly—be not impatient,
(Strong is your hold O mortal flesh,
Strong is your hold O love.)

WALT WHITMAN
"The Last Invocation"

Oh, charming organic beauty not composed of painting or stone but of living corruptible matter. Look at the shoulders and hips and the flowery bosoms on both sides of the chest and the ribs aligned in pairs and the navel in the belly's softness and the dark sex between the thighs! Let me feel your pores exhaling and touch your down, a human image of water and albumen destined to the anatomy of the tomb and let me die with my lips pressed to yours!

> THOMAS MANN
> from *The Magic Mountain*

~

Was this the face that launched a thousand ships
And burst the topless towers of Ilium?
Sweet Helen, make me immortal with a kiss!
Her lips suck forth my soul; see where it flies!
Come Helen, give me my soul again.
Here I will dwell, for Heaven is in these lips . . .

> CHRISTOPHER MARLOWE

*S*till she waited, in her swoon and her drifting, waited, like the Sleeping Beauty in the story. She waited, and again his face was bent to hers, his lips came warm to her face, their footsteps lingered and ceased, they stood still under the trees, whilst his lips waited on her face, waited like a butterfly that does not move on a flower. She pressed her breast a little nearer to him, he moved, put both his arms round her, and drew her close.

And then, in the darkness, he bent to her mouth, softly, and touched her mouth with his mouth. She was afraid, she lay still in his arms, feeling his lips on her lips. She kept still, helpless. Then his mouth drew near, pressing open her mouth, a hot drenching surge rose within her, she opened her lips to him, in pained poignant eddies she drew him nearer, she let him come further, his lips came and surging, surging, soft, so soft, yet oh, like the powerful surge of water, irresistible, till with a little blind cry, she broke away.

D. H. LAWRENCE
from *The Rainbow*

77

What sex is really about is the magic of meeting another person. It isn't so much about orgasm or love as it is about magic. It is a sudden unexpected meeting in which one person gives everything—totally—that can be given by one human being to another. It is about nakedness and it is about mystery. It isn't about what you do together, it is about meeting—a meeting that transcends time, worry and ambition. It is a moment of truth, an unforgettable glimpse of eternity. It is about the transcendence of all the usual parameters through which we relate. The more you try to hold onto your power, influence, and status, the less likely it is that such magic will occur. Letting go of all those safeguards requires courage, of course, but the ultimate gift to yourself and your friend would be to disregard the obstacles and to allow that miracle to transform you.

WILLIAM ASHOKA ROSS

Sweet one for whom I have long sighed,
O cast one loving glance on me!
Though all the world shall frown beside,
Thy love alone my crown should be;
And my devoted, grateful heart
Should turn in rapture unto thee,
If thou wouldst bend those gentle eyes
With tender love and trust on me.
Could such a fate as this be mine,
T'would be a glimpse of love divine,
And never should I seek to gain
Release from love's delicious chain.

VICTORIAN VERSE

Let him kiss me with the kisses of his mouth; for thy love
is better than wine . . .
Thy lips, O my spouse, drop as the honeycomb: honey and milk are
under thy tongue . . .
And the roof of thy mouth like the best wine for my beloved, that
goeth down sweetly, causing the lips of those that are
asleep to speak.

The Song of Solomon

~

There are never enough 'I love you's.

LENNY BRUCE

The Fountains mingle with the River
And the Rivers with the Ocean,
The winds of Heaven mix for ever
With a Sweet Emotion;
Nothing in the world is single;
All things by a law divine
In one spirit met and mingle.
Why not I with Thine?—
See the mountains kiss high Heaven
And the waves clasp one another;
No sister-flower would be forgiven
If it disdained its brother,
And the sunlight claps the earth
And the moonbeams kiss the sea;
What is all this sweet work worth
If thou kiss not me?

PERCY BYSSHE SHELLEY

The high priestess sits at the entrance to the temple, her eyes open and still, her hands folded in her lap. From across the great chessboard plane I approach her. She never looks away, yet never looks at me, never moves, never gives a clue if she notices me or not. I ache to be seen by her, keep moving closer to her, despite her stillness, because of her stillness. As I reach her, she opens her arm to one side, spreading her robe into a curtain, taking me inside, into her temple, the home of wisdom.

Her robe is white and full-flowing, white and rippling with grey shadows. I pass under her arm into the folds, the billowing curtain all around me like wind in high grasses, like smoke in a still room, like Northern lights, like dance. And then there is nothing but the stillness, the stillness and everywhere the magic, which is everything and nothing. All direction is gone: I am snow blind. Even the ground is silken curtain calling, soothing, stroking. I am to be exploded into a million droplets of whatever I have been. I can feel the charge building. I ache to be blown apart, and also I am afraid. Only the texture, and somewhere too a scent, sweet and mysterious—only the texture and the smell of the flowing whiteness keep me from running away.

DAVID STEINBERG
"The High Priestess"

$\mathcal{T}$ry sending an invitation to your beloved for a passionate encounter. You can tuck it in a lunch bag, tape it to the bathroom mirror, slip it under a pillow, or even fax it to the office. To avoid scandal, you can make up your own love code or use an acronym popular with American soldiers when writing to their sweethearts during the two world wars:

Norwich: [K]NICKERS OFF READY WHEN I COME HOME

Burma: BE UNDRESSED AND READY, MY ANGEL

Egypt: EAGER TO GRAB YOUR PRETTY TITS (OR TOES)

Come to me with / magic / glowing on your flesh
I am here, I am here where I always am
flowers in my hair, small orange lilies that
cry out for joy when they lie crushed between us
anointing our bodies with their perfumed lives
come to me, I am here, here where I always am
threading the stars that hang in the branches of the sky
shaping a garland of light for a love-gift
weaving a rose of glory to bloom in your misty hair
come to me through the corridors of night
where green girls dance
spinning their shadows into dreams
let your hands be as birds
and let them fly over me
I will take your breath as the summer wind
and I will give you that which I am
the gardens of my body
and the star-plains of my mind
be as the sun, and I will be the moon
and we will dance the iridescent skies
until the universe becomes one total pulse of joy
and neither lover nor beloved do exist
but only love

LENORE KANDEL
"Witch/Song"

Are you ready for meaningful, heart-moving contact? Then decide that together with your beloved, you're going to create a fun little space capsule of love energy as often as you can. How do you do that? You warmly hold your partner's hands, look steadily into his or her eyes—and smile! The smile is what does it. There are all kinds of smiles, and you can try out all of them. Stay together like this for a few minutes; continue looking, go on holding hands, and keep smiling. Creating this endearing little island of love energy from time to time will reconnect you with your soul mate in a very warm and positive way.

WILLIAM ASHOKA ROSS

*T*rue love needs the foundation of physical affection. Bodies not only house our spirits, they express our spirits. They communicate, without words, the essence of our beings.

When we were babies, we received the feeling of being loved through the sensations we felt in the presence of our parents' bodies. Being nestled next to your mother's heart, being lifted and carried in your father's strong arms—these were the physical sensations that have given us a sense of security and made us feel loved.

If you received the blessings of physical kindness and attention from your parents, these are feelings you wish to return to, and if you never received such nurturance and affection, this is a state you long to finally arrive at.

When our bodies are joyous, our emotions are positive and spirits are uplifted. Therefore, the gift of your beloved's body, more than anything else, can make you feel loved.

So be generous with your body, and not only when you're making love. Give each other a foot massage or a back rub. Prepare a cool washcloth for a fevered brow, or a mud pack for a bee sting. Wrap an ace bandage around a sprained ankle. Be the bearer of Band-Aids, soup and medicines. Kiss for no reason; allow your warmhearted hug of greeting to become a deep embrace. Let your hand brush the shoulder of your beloved when you pass by her in the kitchen. Touch his woolly arm when you sit beside him on the couch. Let the curve of her foot make your foot less lonely while you fall asleep. When he's brokenhearted, touch his face; when she is discouraged, hold her head like a precious bowl between two hands.

Let your bodies speak your truth. Make love with the consciousness that your body can say what you cannot, and know that in this sensuous abandon sexual passion is the dancing of the spirit.

DAPHNE ROSE KINGMA

*N*ot a word!
The eyes speak in rivers,
    the fingers in trees.
The body has a language all its own:
this time we will send the interpreter home.

I will open you
    petal by petal
    taking all the time in the world.
I will build with you a slow fire
    stick by stick
    and watch the color of your sunrise
I will play with the wind of you,
    cover your body with smiles and games,
    promises and fantasies that disappear
    without a trace.
I will stir your secret core,
    witch's brew of potions and incantations,
    and feel you simmering, rolling,
    floating in my hand.
I will fill you slowly up,
every crevice and curve,
watch feel hear smell taste you
growing full.

And when every part of you is one,
when you are saturated, suspended,
water trembling over the brim,
I will ride with you over the falls
    drown with you
    disappear all boundaries
tumble over and over
    and over and over
until there is only the spinning dizzy
dance beyond dancing
and the great wave crashing to bits
everything, leaving us
strewn with the seaweed
in the sand and the sun
to dry.

DAVID STEINBERG
"To Whom It May Concern"

When she rises in the morning
I linger to watch her;
She spreads the bath-cloth underneath the window
And the sunbeams catch her
Glistening white on the shoulders,
While down her sides the mellow
Golden shadow glows as
She stoops to the sponge, and her swung breasts
Sway like full-blown yellow
Gloire de Dijon roses.

She drips herself with water, and her shoulders
Glisten as silver, they crumple up
Like wet and falling roses, and I listen
For the sluicing of their rain-dishevelled petals.
In the window full of sunlight
Concentrates her golden shadow
Fold on fold, until it glows as
Mellow as the glory roses.

D. H. LAWRENCE
"Gloire de Dijon"

Wild Nights—Wild Nights!
Were I with thee
Wild Nights should be
Our luxury!

Futile—the Winds—
To a Heart in port—
Done with the Compass—
Done with the Chart!

Rowing in Eden—
Ah, the Sea!
Might I but moor—Tonight—
In Thee!

EMILY DICKINSON

Within twenty-four hours of the time you wish to make love, sit before a red candle with a red rose in water.
Breathe deeply, in and out, slowly quieting your body.
Concentrate on your heart center.
Visualize this red energy penetrating your heart and flowing into your hands.
Allow the energy also to flow into your pelvis.
Keep this vision going, breathing in and out and allowing the red energy to pulse into your hands and pelvis.

Allow the energy to stay in your body.

SAY ALOUD:
    Within the mystery of the elements
    I accept the fire of passion,
    the pool of my love,
    the atmosphere of romance,
    in the earth of my body.
    I hold this energy and draw on it in a physical manifestation of love.

With gratitude for this pleasure, I say
So be it.
And so it is.

Use the candle and the rose for atmosphere.

BARRIE DOLNICK
Energetic Practices for Passion

~

*L*ady with lotus eyes,
Reclining on your bed of leaves,
Untie your belt,
Let fall your petticoat,
And part your pretty thighs
That he who loves you may delight
In gazing on your hidden jewel.

JAYADEVA
from *Gitagovindam*

93

*C*ome, Madam, come, all rest my powers defy,
Until I labour, I in labour lie.
The foe oft-times having the foe in sight
Is tired with standing though he never fight.
Off with that girdle, like heaven's zone glittering,
But a far fairer world encompassing.
Unpin that spangled breastplate which you wear,
That th'eyes of busy fools may be stopped there.
Unlace yourself, for that harmonious chime
Tells me from you that now it is bed time.
Off with that happy busk, which I envy,
That still can be, and still can stand so nigh.
Your gown going off such beauteous state reveals
As when from flow'ry meads th'hill's shadow steals.
Off with that wiry coronet and show
The hairy diadem which on you doth grow:
Now off with those shoes, and then safely tread
In this love's hallow'd temple, this soft bed.
In such white robes, heaven's angels us'd to be
Receiv'd by men; thou angel bring'st with thee
A heaven like Mahomet's paradise; and though
Ill spirits walk in white, we easily know
By these angels from an evil sprite,
Those set our hairs, but these our flesh upright.
License my roving hands, and let them go,
Before, behind, between, above, below.

O my America! my new-found-land,
My kingdom, safliest when with one man mann'd,
My mine of precious stones, my empery,
How blest am I in this discovering thee!
To enter in these bonds, is to be free;
Then where my hand is set, my seal shall be.
Full nakedness! All joys are due to thee,
As souls unbodied, bodies uncloth'd must be,
To taste whole joys. Gems which you women use
Are like Atlanta's balls, cast in men's views,
That when a fool's eye lighteth on a gem,
His earthly soul may covet theirs, not them.
Like pictures, or like books' gay coverings made
For lay-men, are all women thus array'd;
Themselves are mystic books, which only we
(Whom their imputed grace will dignify)
Must see reveal'd. Then since that I may know,
As liberally, as to a midwife, show
Thy self: cast all, yea, this white linen hence,
There is no penance due to innocence.
To teach thee, I am naked first; why then
What need'st thou have more covering than a man?

JOHN DONNE
"Elegy: On His Mistress Going To Bed"

95

How beautiful are thy feet with shoes, O prince's daughter! The joints of thy thighs are like jewels, the work of the hands of a cunning workman. Thy navel is like a round goblet, which wanteth not liquor: thy belly is like a heap of wheat set about with lilies. Thy two breasts are like two young roes that are twins. Thy neck is as a tower of ivory: thine eyes like the fishpools in Heshbon, by the gate of Bathrabbim: thy nose is as the tower of Lebanon which looketh toward Damascus. Thine head upon thee is like Carmel, and the hair of thine head like purple: the King is held in the galleries. How fair and how pleasant art thou, O love, for delights! This thy stature is like to a palm tree, and thy breasts to clusters of grapes. I said, I will go up to the palm tree, I will take hold of the boughs thereof: now also thy breasts shall be as clusters of the vine, and the smell of thy nose like apples; And the roof of thy mouth like the best wine for my beloved, that goeth down sweetly, causing the lips of those that are asleep to speak.

The Song of Solomon

*I*f you enjoy your food, you can learn to really enjoy sex. If you gulp your food or eat yourself into oblivion, you won't. If you eat mostly in fast-food places and flush down hamburgers and fries with soda pop, your openness to the sensory spectrum will diminish. It's your choice! You can eat strawberries so that you get a full taste by slicing them, which is a sensory experience. Or you can simply swallow them whole, in which case all that happens is that you ingest some nutrition.

It's all a question of how open you are to sensations. How much *pleasure* do you allow yourself? When you take a shower, do you let yourself enjoy it? Or is it merely a means to an end? All of that carries over into sex. If you take that means-to-an-end approach, soon there won't be any end that really satisfies—and not much sex either that's worth anything.

WILLIAM ASHOKA ROSS

The lighting in the bedroom, natural or otherwise, changes the mood, and candles provide the perfect illumination for romance. try burning a peach-colored candle, because peach has a stabilizing effect that helps to provide a calm atmosphere. It resonates comfort, safety, and well-being. Peach will reassure your lover that you are trustworthy and that you only have eyes for him or her.

Your senses are very important, and how you cater to them makes a very big difference in your life. You don't want to fall asleep in your bedroom every night because your senses are exhausted or bored. Be creative in your bedroom; cast spells before going to sleep, meditate, or do some yoga stretches. Keep excitement brewing there.

ZSUZSANNA E. BUDAPEST
The Goddess in the Bedroom

All night our room was outer-walled with rain.
Drops fell and flattened on the tin roof,
And rang like little disks of metal.
Ping!—Ping!—and there was not a pinpoint of silence
between them.
The rain rattled and clashed,
And the slats of the shutters danced and glittered.
But to me the darkness was red-gold and
crocus-coloured
With your brightness,
And the words you whispered to me
Sprang up and flamed—orange torches against the rain.
Torches against the wall of cool, silver rain.

AMY LOWELL
"Summer Rain"

Tantric texts state that a woman's upper lip is one of the most erogenous parts of her body. They believe this special sensitivity is due to a subtle nerve channel that connects her upper lip to her clitoris. "A man can stimulate the woman's upper lip by gently nibbling and sucking, while she plays with his lower lip with her teeth and tongue," write Nik Douglas and Penny Slinger in *Sexual Secrets*. "If the teeth are carefully controlled to create waves of pleasure rather than pain, this practice can be very arousing for both partners."

~

What I love about sex is that it is never completed. You think it is finished and you realize you never get there. It's as a prism.

ANICA VESEL MANDER

Sit facing your partner and relax. With your left palm facing up and your right palm facing down, allow your palms and your partner's to gently rest on one another. Looking into his or her eyes, softly say the words, "I am letting go." As you do this, move your joined hands slowly in unison, so that as your right hand moves forward, your left hand is moving backward and vice-versa. Your partner validates your affirmation by saying, "You are letting go."

Take your time with this. Again and again look into your partner's eyes and softly say, "I am letting go" or "I am finally letting go." Breathe easily and effortlessly as you do this. When it feels right to you, allow your eyes to close and continue making these declarations. Do this for about 10–15 minutes.

WILLIAM ASHOKA ROSS

Enticing
Interludes

"My body is a candle touched by fire."
RUMI

$\mathscr{S}$exuality becomes an evermore beautiful vocabulary when we allow it to include sensuality. Sensuality is the delicious gratuitousness of making love, the unnecessary but wonderful play of all the senses—touch, sight, smell, hearing and taste—in the sexual encounter.

Expressing sensuality is an elevation of the interaction, an invitation for us to become more fully human, to live from our instinctual sensing selves as well as our rational thinking selves. So it is that when you make love through the richness of your sensuality, you may receive through the body of your beloved the whole complex beauty of his or her incarnation.

By being generous with your sensuality, with your beautifully intoxicating words, in beholding the grace, the strength of the body you cherish, breathing its fragrance, tasting its essence, you will also nourish each other's souls.

DAPHNE ROSE KINGMA

$\mathscr{S}$uddenly Will runs in to me, wearing his motley. He turns for me, showing it off. He drops his mask, then puts it back on, doing a little dance around the room, miming the perfect Harlequin. Then all at once he banishes the maids in a stern, masterly voice. They flee from the room bowing and tittering. My heart pounds as if it should fly out of my bosom. Then it happens—all in a rush—he takes me in his arms (I still dressed in my boy's doublet), holds me fast, and kisses me with molten sweetness.

"Jessica, Jessica," he says, enfolding me. The tight rosebud between my thighs, furled for so many celibate months, wants nothing more than to explode, but my mind races ahead as minds will. Perhaps when animals mate it is all a matter of blood and nerves, scents and synapses, vessels filling and vessels emptying (although sometimes I doubt even that); but humans love within the context of that great convention "Love," that well-worn metaphor "Love," that gaudy tapestry "Love" woven through the ages by the poets and artists, dyed in our nerves, imprinted on our brains, accompanied by sweet familiar music.

Oh, I had loved and lusted, loved and "Loved." And sometimes I was not sure whether I had loved "Love" or the man in question, myself and my role as Inamorata, or just the adrenaline rush of love, that most powerful of all drugs, that highest of all highs— kickier than cocaine, more euphoric than opium, dizzier than dope. For sometimes we create a lover out of a parti-colored fool just to feel that rush again—and when the rush is over, we look at him and laugh, asking ourselves why.

But at its truest, love is altogether another matter: a matter of gods and goddesses, or spirits merging, of a holy communion in the flesh. And one never knows, before making that leap of faith, whether one will find pure spirit or mere motley, holy communion or sexual aerobics, gods and goddesses, or goat and monkeys. "Who chooseth me must give and hazard all he hath"— the essence and the test of love.

ERICA JONG
from *Serenissima*

On a Tuesday during a waxing moon,
in the fifth hour of darkness:

Together, light two red candles
and two pink candles.
Touch each candle with the scent of
rose, lavender, or musk.

Give each other flowers:
violets
daisies
hibiscus

Give each other a glass of water.

Sit together before the flames.
Breathe in and out, quietly feeling your energies
mingle.

SAY ALOUD TOGETHER:
    We honor the fires of passion.
    We welcome the lightness of air.

We enjoy the pleasures of the earth.
We drink the warmth of love.

Enjoy the evening.

> BARRIE DOLNICK
> *Spell to Share the Passion*

~

One of the ways to have great sex is to delay sexual gratification while raising your sexual energy. Tantric teachers suggest connecting sexually for ten minutes every day for a week without having an orgasm. On the seventh day, "go all the way" and see how ecstatic it feels. But be sure to practice for ten minutes each day!

$\mathscr{I}$ remember the preacher said: "Let them be joined together forever in the Holy Spirit," and I kind of wrinkled my brow because God is easy and Jesus is easy but the Holy Spirit thing was always way beyond me, and I wasn't really sure that what I had in mind was a ménage à trois with some supposedly benevolent essence, and in my poor agnostic head I imagined the two of us suspended in the spiritual plasma of the Holy Ghost for eternity like watermelon pickles.

But when we headed out of the old adobe church that day so far as I could tell it was still the two of us, just you and me, light-headed as teenagers in the summer in the evening in the park, our vows an exotic narcotic wrapped in plastic and shoved down deep in our socks.

And I remember we didn't even make love that night, but consummated our marriage in the deep sweet of sleep. In the morning there were tiny roses of blood on the bed and I knew that my dreams had ferried across the occult water of sleep and with a broad flat sword had broken through the soft dense flesh of your maidenhead to dance with you to the beat of feral drums.

And when the morning had come, sure enough, there was the Holy Spirit, less like a poltergeist and more like a cat, perched on a comforter on the old steamer trunk at the end of the bed.

"Go ahead," the Holy Spirit dared me. "Touch her." And I touched you and the walls shuddered like an old miner's shack teetering into the San Andreas fault.

"Holy shit," I said, thinking this could be dangerous, and then I realized that I had blasphemed and I was afraid and embarrassed.

"It's okay," the Holy Spirit told me. "You go right ahead. Don't worry. Nothing can harm you."

So I kissed your ear, and Aretha Franklin began to sing.

And I pulled off your T-shirt and the bed danced a samba across the floor.

And you said "that's cool," and I said "you try it" and you kissed me on the lips and instantaneously the bedroom walls shattered, covering us in gypsum dust and little puffs of pink insulation and bright shards of glass.

I cupped your breast in my hand and bit at your nipple and the trees moaned with pleasure and all the neighborhood children gathered around us in the rubble and danced in a ring, their little hands holding each other gingerly like hamsters.

I touched your belly and Gideon appeared, his trumpet blasting a Hallelujah into the quivering sky.

Then you pulled hard at my back and fire roared down from the sky like napalm, sucking the air from my lungs and smoldering in jellied splotches on the soles of my feet.

I stroked your side and buck naked laughing seraphim appeared fluttering all around me, randomly shooting morphine-dipped arrows into my butt.

Light stuck to your naked body like a fresh-cut haystack after a rain. You looked just like a desert sunrise and you tasted just like filé gumbo and you smelled just like the spray from the breakers at Patrick's Point.

Puppies played under your skin and some unseen hand snaked a length of hairy twine up from my tailbone and out through the center of my skull, harmlessly pulling out bits of unused brain tissue that stuck to my hair like marshmallows.

And when I pulled your thighs apart the sky opened and God himself came thundering down wearing a porkpie hat with a press pass stuck in it, taking a seat at the announcer's desk of some celestial sky box, surrounded on every side by bleachers full of rowdy drunken angels.

"Don't mind Me," He said into the microphone.

And then He filled us so full of the Holy Spirit that It oozed out of us and we slipped and slid across each other, the Holy Spirit sticky in our mouths, the Holy Spirit leaking liquid blue light from our fingertips, the Holy Spirit trickling down our foreheads and stinging into our eyes, the Holy Spirit pouring from our armpits and off our legs and our shoulders and from between your legs and making a holy mess on the bed.

We were speaking in tongues. We were rolling holy rolling in the sheets. Our tongues were driven mad with Pentecostal ecstasy, our tongues were epileptic, our tongues were frothing, our tongues were crying, our tongues were screaming, our tongues were babbling holy nonsense, our tongues were baptized, our tongues were washed with the Blood of the Lamb, and our tongues were born again. And again.

And as our tongues gave witness to the power of the Holy Spirit, I heard the strange words rise up into Heaven and rattle the very cage of the universe, building, like an argument, shattered, like the Tower of Babel, resurrected, like Jesus, emerging from the dark cave of our souls.

And then it was night again, and the Holy Spirit settled down on us like a feather comforter, a soft weight that pulled us close in the night, down toward the dark beat of drums around a fire in the forest along turgid river of sleep.

And as I drifted slowly down from the headwaters of consciousness, I remembered what the preacher said: "Let them be joined together forever in the Holy Spirit," and I pulled you closer and murmured from my tired, tired tongue, "oh, baby, amen."

CARSON REED
"Speaking in Tongues"

~

Each evening the sea casts starfish up on the beach, scattering, stranding them. They die at dawn, leaving black hungers in the sun. We slept there that summer, we fucked in their radiant evolutions up to our body. Ringed by starfish gasping for their element, we joined to create ours. All night they inhaled the sweat from our thrusting limbs, and lived. Often she cried out: Your hand!—It was a starfish, caressing her with my low fire.

BILL KNOT (ST. GERAUD)

'Twas a new feeling—something more
Than we had dared to own before,
    Which then we hid not;
We saw it in each other's eye,
And wished, in every half-breathed sigh,
    To speak, but did not.

She felt my lips' impassioned touch—
'Twas the first time I dared so much,
    And yet she chid not;
But whispered o'er my burning brow,
'Oh, do you doubt I love you now?'
    Sweet soul! I did not.

Warmly I felt her bosom thrill,
I pressed it closer, closer still,
    Though gently bid not;
Till—oh! the world hath seldom heard
Of lovers, who so nearly erred,
    And yet, who did not.

             THOMAS MOORE
             "Did Not"

In the space of my life I design such rooms:
I trim the air to music's measurements; I start
a fire in the fire's place; you are secure
in the double-chambered neighborhood
of loving, and the whole house raises
its cain of distinct
possibilities. Let us
have our differences: let go

wildness from its hold, the buzz and heat
of pleasure from its separate cells. The sweetness
is of paradox, intact, untouched, in the couch
of an accommodating hearth, in the nightlong
red-hot beehive we have started.

HEATHER MCHUGH
"Domestic Song"

She was nearly at the wide riding when he came up and flung his naked arm round her soft, naked-wet middle. She gave a shriek and straightened herself, and the heap of her soft, chill flesh came up against his body. He pressed it all up against him, madly, the heap of soft, chilled, female flesh that became quickly warm as flame, in contact. The rain streamed on them till they smoked. He gathered her lovely, heavy posteriors one in each hand and pressed them in towards him in a frenzy, quivering motionless in the rain. Then suddenly he tipped her up and fell with her on the path, in the roaring silence of the rain, and short and sharp, he took her, short and sharp and finished, like an animal.

D. H. LAWRENCE
from *Lady Chatterley's Lover*

Take my hand. There are two of us in this cave.
The sound you hear is water: you will hear it forever.
The ground you walk on is rock. I have been here
before.
People come here to be born, to discover, to kiss,
to dream and to dig and to kill. Watch for the mud.
Summer blows in with scent of horses and roses;
fall with the sound of sound breaking; winter shoves
its empty sleeve down the dark of your throat.
You will learn toads from diamonds, the fist from the
palm,
love from the sweat of love, falling from flying.
There are a thousand turnoffs. I have been here
before.
Once I fell off a precipice. Once I found gold.
Once I stumbled on murder, the thin parts of a girl.
Walk on, keep walking, there are axes above us.
Watch for occasional bits and bubbles of light—
birthdays for you, recognitions: *yourself, another.*
Watch for the mud. Listen for bells, for beggars.
Something with wings went crazy against my chest
once.
There are two of us here. Touch me.

> LISEL MUELLER
> "The Blind Leading the Blind"

How can one woman's skin hold so much light?
When my mouth brushes across the silken
desert of your belly, blossoms ignite
in copper sparks beneath my tongue, darken
in certain curves to caramel. You invite
me deeper, where I can feel you open,
sense the heat adobe holds nearing night.

I sing of apricot and brass. Hidden
coals glow sienna, almost out of sight,
stoked by my hands and breath, by my brazen
heart which flickers in this landscape despite
those who hiss I should not touch a woman
here, and here. Yes. Pull down the stars tonight.

> PAMELA CROW
> "Here"

119

Lying back beside her, Martin slipped off his pants. Martin's feet had gone aquatic, giving themselves to the air like an ocean polyp. There was no resistance. Annie slid over the spread and put her mouth firmly over Martin's longing sex. She held onto it lightly and strongly, like a snake with a very small pig.

Salad talk from the summer before and the summer before that. Especially in New Mexico where the zucchini came to be enormous, so big that they grew out of their flavor and left only an arctic interior for disappointed faces. By then we'd run out of any new ways to cook the things. Laura's recipe of shredding and sautéing was the best. And everyone could eat this without too many complaints in full view of the mesa, late August lightning storms, violent and very far off.

Martin was a man whose sex was sweetly compatible with her face. Annie began to ride. She pinched her buttocks together, pressing the bell between her legs against the bed. It was a hammock swing held tight and blown from side to side.

Really she didn't think of it as pleasure. That was such a weak expression. Pleasure was just an idea about experience. Her love for the sexual part of her being was as familiar and surprising as watching her random fingers move up and down. Now she let those fingers slip over the smooth insides of Martin's thighs. Find their way back under his well-used sit bones and knead the soft-pressed behind. Everything was working harder and faster. Her fingers digging under and around stretching the two cheeks apart. Annie's mouth strangled his sex. Her whole body in long motion and her fingers at it too. A small stream of that early melon juice ran down him and over her lips.

SUMMER BRENNER
from *The Soft Room*

121

$\mathcal{S}$ex is the ultimate intimacy, the ultimate touching when, like two paramecia, we engulf one another. We play at devouring each other, digesting each other, we nurse on each other, drink each other's fluids, get under each other's skin. Kissing, we share one breath, open the sealed fortress of our body to our lover. We shelter under a warm net of kisses. We drink from the well of the other's body, we map the new terrain with our fingertips and lips, pausing at the oasis of a nipple, the hillock of a thigh, the backbone's meandering riverbed. It is a kind of pilgrimage of touch, which leads to the temple of our desire.

DIANE ACKERMAN

When looking to spice up your sex life, don't overlook the nose. From time immemorial, scents have been used to create erotic delights. Historically, olfactory aphrodisiacs include amber, ambergris, civetone, jasmine, lily of the valley, musk, myrrh, orange blossom, patchouli, sandalwood, and tuberose. Contemporary "erotically oriented" perfumes include Eau Sauvage, Magic Noire, and Poison, each of which contains some of these ancient aphrodisiacs. One Tantric ritual suggests placing different scents on various parts of the body: oil of spikenard (you'll need a substitute—it's found only in the Himalayas) for hair, patchouli for cheeks and breasts, jasmine for hands, saffron for feet and musk for pubic hair. You might also try perfuming the bedroom with night-blooming jasmine or tuberoses. Or burn some incense.

Tandem touching is an exercise that is highly useful. It takes about an hour. Take turns touching each other so that while one lover is the receiver, the other lover is the donor. After half an hour or so, switch roles.

The receiver is always in charge and can say, "No I don't want you to touch me like that; I want you to touch me like this"—more softly, more gently, whatever the case may be. Keep in mind that in the first week or two of this exercise, genitals and nipples should not be touched.

The key to tandem touching is to do it over a long period of time—several times a week for at least a month. All sorts of strange feelings will arise, but if you hang in there, it will be worthwhile. It's very important that you resist the temptation to have intercourse, because that would abort the gradual buildup of sensations that is possible with this exercise.

WILLIAM ASHOKA ROSS

One day Daniel showed me an old [illustrated] Chinese Taoist pillow book he had found in Hawaii. . . .

[A] favorite was a bathing picture that Daniel and I decided to re-create every weekend. During the week I bought lavender soap, loofah sponges, and an East Indian bubble elixir that turned the bath an enchanting blue. He brought volcanic pumice stone for my feet, his mother's homemade tropical shampoo for my hair, and coconut massage oil for my sunburned skin. He made a life-size topographical map of my body, naming his favorite places after mountains and valleys he'd studied on maps of the ancient world. I wrote him primitive poetry, then recited it in our bath as we faced one another, encircled by candles. In our glowing water cave, we were two initiates, learning the luxurious language of touch and time.

BRENDA PETERSON

$\mathcal{U}$ntil the very moment that our naked bodies touched in that old brass bed that creaked in the insulated sunporch on Walker Road, I had no idea what I was doing there, nor what I wanted to do there. I had no idea what making love to another woman meant.

I only knew, dimly, it was something I wanted to happen, and something that was different from anything I had ever done before.

I reached out and put an arm around Ginger, and through the scents of powder and soap and hand cream I could smell the rising flush of her own spicy heat. I took her into my arms, and she became precious beyond compare. I kissed her on the mouth, this time with no thought at all. My mouth moved to the little hollow beneath her ear.

Ginger's breath warmed my neck and started to quicken. My hands moved down over her round body, silky and fragrant, waiting. Uncertainty and doubt rolled away from the mouth of my wanting like a great stone, and my unsureness dissolved in the directing heat of my own frank and finally open desire.

Our bodies found the movements we needed to fit each other.

Ginger's flesh was sweet and moist and firm as a winter pear. I felt her and tasted her deeply, my hands and my mouth and my whole body moved against her. Her flesh opened to me like a peony and the unfolding depths of her pleasure brought me back to her body over and over again throughout the night. The tender nook between her legs, moist and veiled with thick crispy dark hair.

I dove beneath her wetness, her fragrance, the silky insistence of her body's rhythms illuminating my own hungers. We rode each other's need. Her body answered the quest of my fingers my tongue my desire to know a woman, again and again, until she arced like a rainbow, and surfaced dizzy and blessed with her rich myrrh-taste in my mouth, in my throat, smeared over my face, and the loosening grip of her hands in my hair and the wordless sounds of her satisfaction lulling me like a song.

Once, as she cradled my head between her breasts, Ginger whispered, "I could tell you knew how," and the pleasure and satisfaction in her voice started my tides flowing again and I moved down against her once more, my body upon hers, ringing like a bell.

I never questioned where my knowledge of her body and her need came from. Loving Ginger that night was like coming home to a joy I was meant for, and I only wondered, silently, how I had not always

127

known that it would be so. Ginger moved in love like she laughed, openly and easily, and I moved with her, against her, an ocean of brown warmth. Her sounds of delight and the deep shudders of relief that rolled through her body in the wake of my strolling fingers filled me with delight and a hunger for more of her. The sweetness of her body meeting and filling my mouth, my hands wherever I touched, felt right and completing, as if I had been born to make love to this woman, and was remembering her body rather than learning it deeply for the first time.

In wonder, but without surprise, I lay finally quiet with my arms around Ginger. So this was what I had been so afraid of not doing properly. How ridiculous and far away those fears seemed now, as if loving were some task outside of myself, rather than simply reaching out and letting my own desire guide me. It was all so simple. I felt so good I smiled into the darkness. Ginger cuddled closer.

AUDRE LORDE
from ZAMI: A New Spelling of My Name

$\mathcal{W}$hen you and your lover are ready to enter into the dance of sexual loving together, when it is time to leave the separate worlds of your two bodies and join them as one, your reunion will begin with touch. Deep within you, a longing stirs—to feel the form of your beloved beneath your fingers, to feel the heat of his flesh next to yours, as if to reassure yourself that he is real, that your love is real. You may not even have the conscious thought, "I need to touch him," but your heart has spoken, and your body will listen.

From within the boundaries of your physical universe, your hand reaches out and travels across the space that separates you and your lover, the space that defines you as two, until suddenly, your hand makes contact with its destination—an arm, a thigh, a face, another hand, and *instantly, everything is different.* You are touching the outer edges of your partner's world. You can feel him in there, all of him, beyond the doorway of his skin. You will never get to physically touch the totality of the formless being housed inside, but for now, this is enough. The connection has been made, and its solidity reassures you that you are not alone.

BARBARA DE ANGELIS

Behind naming, beneath words, is something else. An existence named unnamed, and unnameable. We give the grass a name, and earth a name. We say grass and earth are separate. We know this because we can pull grass free of the earth and see its separate roots–but when the grass is free, it dies. We say the inarticulate have no souls. We say the cow's eye has no existence outside ourselves, that the red wing of the blackbird has no thought, the roe of the salmon no feeling, because we cannot name these. Yet for our own lives we grieve all that cannot be spoken, that there is no name for, repeating for ourselves the names of things which surround what cannot be named. We say Heron and Loon, Coot and Killdeer, Snipe and Sandpiper, Gull and Hawk, Eagle and Osprey, Pigeon and Dove, Oriole, Meadowlark, Sparrow. We say Red Admiral and Painted Lady, Morning Cloak and Question Mark, Baltimore and Checkerspot, Buckeye, Monarch, Viceroy, Mayfly, Stonefly, Cicada, Leafhopper and Earwig, we say Sea Urchin and Sand Dollar, Starfish and Sandworm. We say mucous membrane, uterus, cervix, ligament, vagina and hymen, labia, orifice, artery, vessel, spine and heart. We say skin, blood, breast, nipple, taste, nostril, green,

eye, hair, we say vulva, hood, clitoris, belly, foot, knee,
elbow, pit, nail, thumb, we say tongue, teeth, toe, ear, we
say ear and voice and touch and taste and we say again
love, breast and beautiful and vulva, saying clitoris, saying
belly, saying toes and soft, saying ear, saying ear, saying
ear and saying hood and hood and green and all that we
say we are saying around that which cannot be said,
cannot be spoken. But in a moment that which is behind
naming makes itself known. Hand and breast know each
one to the other. Wood in the table knows clay in the bowl.
Air knows grass knows water knows mud knows beetle
knows frost knows sunlight knows the shape of the earth
knows death knows not dying. And all this knowledge is in
the souls of everything, behind naming, before speaking,
beneath words.

SUSAN GRIFFIN

Her body is not so white as
anemone petals nor so smooth—nor
so remote a thing. It is a field
of the wild carrot taking
the field by force; the grass
does not raise above it.
Here is not question of whiteness,
white as can be, with a purple mole
at the center of each flower.
Each flower is a hand's span
of her whiteness. Wherever
his hand has lain there is
a tiny purple blemish. Each part
is a blossom under his touch
to which the fibres of her being
stem one by one, each to its end,
until the whole field is a
white desire, empty, a single stem,
a cluster, flower by flower,
a pious wish to whiteness gone over—
or nothing.

WILLIAM CARLOS WILLIAMS
"Queen Anne's Lace"

$\mathscr{B}$reathing can have a tremendous effect on sex. The deeper the breathing, the more complete the sexual experience. That's why some people say that relaxed and gentle breathing is the gateway to sexual ease. In fact, breathing can by itself lead to ecstasy. That's because ecstasy would be our natural state if our breathing weren't so shallow. Our present energy is actually only a fraction of what it could be. Take a few deep breaths during making love and you'll soon see.

WILLIAM ASHOKA ROSS

133

They would stand sometimes folded together in the barn, in silence. Then to her, as she felt his young, tense figure with her hands, the bliss was intolerable, intolerable the sense that she possessed him. For his body was so keen and wonderful, it was the only reality in her world. In her world, there was this one tense, vivid body of a man, and then many other shadowy men, all unreal. In him, she touched the centre of reality. And they were together, he and she, at the heart of the secret. How she clutched him to her, his body the central body of all life. Out of the rock of his form the very fountain of life flowed.

But to him, she was a flame that consumed him. The flame flowed up his limbs, flowed through him, till he was consumed, till he existed only as an unconscious, dark transit of flame, deriving from her.

D. H. LAWRENCE
from *The Rainbow*

$\mathscr{I}$ remember the time a friend picked a ripe apple from his tree, took a bite from its firm flesh, and offered it to me to sample. We were not lovers. But, biting into the crater his teeth had just left, I joined him in the apple's flesh, which tasted sweet, sex-wet, and open. In that small oasis, our mouths met. Now when I see a photograph of such an apple, I don't think of Mom, Country, and Apple Pie. The image is tinged with the erotic. I think *kiss*.

DIANE ACKERMAN

Making love doesn't exist in a category by itself. When you enter the sacred circle of sexual intimacy, you are inviting yourself to partake of a profound emotional relationship, a spiritual encounter.

To treat sex as anything less is to short-change yourself and, unwittingly, to bring yourself into the presence of nameless sorrow.

Indeed, making love is a form of worship for your incarnation. It is a way of acknowledging in the presence of another human being that we have all come here in a form that longs to engage with one another. In making love we are attracted, drawn to; momentarily, we experience union, are fulfilled. We are overjoyed by one another, time and time again.

Making love is pleasure and passion, and compassion; affection, attention, and consolation. But it is more. It is coming face-to-face with the reality of being human, of being spirit enthralled by physical form. Through it we sing a thanksgiving simply for being alive, for possessing a body, and for that fact that in this life, we do not travel entirely alone.

So honor your sexuality as the mysterious and beautiful power that it is, and it will give back to you more than you ever imagined.

DAPHNE ROSE KINGMA

*N*aked she lay, clasped in my longing arms,
I filled with love, and she all over charms;
Both equally inspired with eager fire,
Melting through kindness, flaming in desire.
With arms, legs lips close clinging to embrace,
She clips me to her breast, and sucks me to her face.
Her nimble tongue, Love's lesser lightning, played
Within my mouth, and to my thoughts conveyed
Swift orders that I should prepare to throw
The all-dissolving thunderbolt below.
My fluttering soul, sprung with the pointed kiss,
Hangs hovering o'er her balmy brinks of bliss.
But whilst her busy hand would guide that part
Which should convey to my soul up to her heart,
In liquid raptures I dissolve all o'er,
Melt into sperm, and spend at every pore.

JOHN WILMOT, EARL OF ROCHESTER
"The Imperfect Enjoyment"

137

$\mathcal{P}$eer of gods he seemeth to me, the blissful
Man who sits and gazes at thee before him,
Close beside thee sits, and in silence hears thee
Silverly speaking,
Laughing love's low laughter. Oh this, this only
Stirs the troubled heart in my breast to tremble!
For should I but see thee a little moment,
Straight is my voice hushed;
Yea, my tongue is broken, and through and through me
'Neath the flesh impalpable fire runs tingling:
Nothing sees my mine eyes, and a noise of roaring
Waves in my ear sounds;
Sweat runs down in rivers, a tremor seizes
All my limbs, and paler than grass in autumn,
Caught by pains of menacing death, I falter,
Lost in the love-trance.

SAPPHO

The first step in touching your partner with love is to *find the love you feel for him or her inside yourself.* You might take a moment before you begin to make love, close your eyes, and think about how much you care for this wonderful person. Focus your awareness on all of the things you adore about him, all of the joy she has brought into your life. Don't get trapped in your mind's collection of hidden grievances or list of imperfections—this isn't the time to concentrate on what's wrong with your partner (a sure turn-off), but rather, to remind yourself what is right about her.

Once you feel the love for your partner in your heart, the second step in practicing loving touch is to move the love energy from your heart into your hands.

BARBARA DE ANGELIS

Strange his wife was to him. It was as if he were a perfect stranger, as if she were infinitely and essentially strange to him, the other half of the world, the dark half of the moon. She waited for his touch as if he were a marauder who had come in, infinitely unknown and desirable to her. And he began to discover her. He had an inkling of the vastness of the unknown sensual store of delights she was. With a passion of voluptuousness that made him dwell on each tiny beauty, in a kind of frenzy of enjoyment, he lit upon her: her beauty, the beauties, the separate, several beauties of her body.

He was quite ousted from himself, and sensually transported by that which he had discovered in her. He was another man revelling over her. There was no tenderness, no love between them anymore, only the maddening, sensuous lust for discovery and the insatiable, exorbitant gratification in the sensual beauties of her body. And she was a store, a store of absolute beauties that it drove him mad to contemplate. There was such a feast to enjoy, and he with only one man's capacity.

He lived in a passion of sensual discovery with her for some time—it was a duel: no love, no words, no kisses even, only the maddening perception of beauty consummate, absolute through touch. He wanted to touch her, to discover her, maddeningly he wanted to know her. Yet he must not hurry, or he missed everything. He must enjoy one beauty at a time. And the multitudinous beauties of her body, the many little rapturous places, sent him mad with delight, and with desire to be able to know more, to have strength to know more. For all was there.

> D. H. LAWRENCE
> from *The Rainbow*

Neither the heart cut by a piece of glass
in a wasteland of thorns
nor the atrocious waters seen in the corners
of certain houses, waters like eyelids and eyes
can capture your waist in my hands
when my heart lifts its oaks
towards your unbreakable thread of snow.

Nocturnal sugar, spirit
of the crowns,
          ransomed
human blood, your kisses
send me into exile
and a stroke of water, with remnants of the sea,
beats on the silences that wait for you
surrounding the worn chairs, wearing out doors.

Nights with bright spindles,
divided, material, nothing
but voice, nothing but
naked every day.

Over your breasts of motionless current,
over your legs of firmness and water,
over the permanence and the pride
of your naked hair

I want to be, my love, now that the tears are
        thrown
into the raucous basket where they accumulate,
I want to be, my love, alone with a syllable
of mangled silver, alone with a tip
of your breast of snow.

PABLO NERUDA
"Pact" (Sonata)

~

Few penises sleep so soundly they cannot be awak-
ened with a kiss—but this kiss is not the peck of a
bird, it is the tongue, palate and lips of a hungry calf
noisily sucking a teat.

JAPANESE PILLOW BOOK

143

Having sensitive hands will do more to make your lover appreciate you than anything else. Everyone is hungry for sensitive, caring, delicate touching. There are many different ways of touching, and you might be surprised by how much there is to learn. Texts like the *Kama Sutra* and *Tibetan Arts of Love* identify five different modalities—embracing (nonmoving), moving (which includes circles, long and short strokes, spirals and other shapes), squeezing (which includes kneading and pinching), scratching, and tapping or slapping (gently!). Each of these can be done at one of seven levels of depth, speed, pressure, and firmness of hands. According to Tantric teachers Charles and Caroline Muir, it's best to alternate firm and soft touch; the brain picks up more feeling when the sensations vary.

"Any movement or touch, even greatly pleasurable ones," they write, "will lose its sensitivity if repeated continually. When you find a good area, leave it . . . and visit it often."

$\mathcal{G}$ood sex depends less on technique than on how appreciative you are. And to be really appreciative means that you are content in the present moment. You don't think about tomorrow, you don't think about the next moment; you're too involved with your feelings in the moment. Obviously, if you're straining for an orgasm, you won't be very appreciative of the moment. You won't pay much attention to what is actually happening. But if you wait to feel appreciative *until* you come, you'll find that you'll have come and gone! Because, as you know, it can all happen in the twinkling of an eye.

WILLIAM ASHOKA ROSS

*J*ust as *coitus* means, really, *to travel together,*
this trip, this movement away from the self
toward the self, this deep delirium of cross-purposes
and unsheathed desires is a journey too:
treacherous, magical, serious, yet also a kind
of substantial gaiety, a dance in which the partners
embrace, separate, and return again to a single
place, in which the other-image ventures out
toward its partner, whom it finds, alters, is
altered by and renews, as wind and sycamore
alter, rectify and renew each other; as the slow,
unalterable turning of the earth alters the galaxies
in some way beyond our seeing. But what are
journeys for, if not to change the very urge that
moves them to begin? And what's marriage if not
a going out that quiets as it moves? Oh, someone
will always be wishing you luck, friends, but luck's
just choice made lucky by repeat, the way a man
thrown overboard makes his own life lucky by

the same stroke time and time again. Why, if I
were God, I'd let these glasses fill again with wine
and luck as Zeus did for that old pair whose only wish
was that they might burn, flicker and go out again as a
single flame. I'd make you oak and linden as they were
and call the shade a silence in your name.
I'd name the birds' embellished song for yours:
a noble thing, this word that's given as the word
        (the vow)
was meant to be, this utterance that love alone makes
        true,
its single light still burning in your eyes.

> MICHAEL BLUMENTHAL
> "Epithalamium: The Single Light"

*N*ot every man has gentians in his house in soft
September, at slow, Sad Michaelmas
Bavarian gentians, big and dark, only dark
darkening the day-time torch-like with the smok-
ing blueness of
Pluto's gloom
ribbed and torch-like, with their blaze of darkness
spread blue
down flattening into points, flattened under the
sweep of white day
torch-flower of the blue-smoking darkness, Pluto's
dark blue daze,
black lamps from the halls of Dis, burning dark
blue,
giving off darkness, blue darkness, as Demeter's
pale lamps give off light,
lead me then, lead me the way.

Reach me a gentian, give me a torch
let me guide myself with the blue, forked torch of
this flower
down the darker and darker stairs, where blue is
darkened on blueness,
even where Persephone goes, just now, from the
frosted September
to the sightless realm where darkness is awake
upon the dark
and Persephone herself is but a voice
or a darkness invisible enfolded in the deeper dark
of the arms Plutonic, and pierced with the passion
of dense gloom,
among the splendour of torches of darkness,
shedding darkness on the lost bride and her groom.

> D. H. LAWRENCE
> "Bavarian Gentians"

Horny means a million things: It means wanting sweat, but also skin, to touch and be touched *anywhere*, to suck and lick, be penetrated, to feel a finger slip between my shirt buttons, and then in between my breasts. Feeling horny is like being pregnant with desire, restless and premonitory, swollen. Predatory, as though I were hunting. I begin to act unseemly, I get reckless, attentive to every person with whom I have the most casual contact. The smallest of meetings shivers with imagined meaning.

Alone in this state I get restless, and watch television, and every show seems laden with entendre, each character on the screen speaking directly to me.

SALLIE TISDALE
from *Talk Dirty to Me*

*I*s anything comparable to the euphoria when your partner sheds those concealing garments and this dazzling body stands revealed, newly sculpted? Suddenly you've come home to that precious world of perpetual nakedness. You look, you touch, and so much starts flowing in you, so many vital juices. Everything becomes liquid, everything stirs. Forbidden fragrances, primeval echoes, haunt the sanctuary your bed has become. You soak up ecstasy through the pores of your skin, and soon you enter a zone of forgetfulness where everything dissolves. Afterward, everything feels fresh, clean, bright and you cry in each other's arms with the sheer joy of it all. And you both know that this is life—not the world of meandering chit-chat, paying bills, and all the rest—but this. Each time is a revelation.

WILLIAM ASHOKA ROSS

*H*er perfume mixes with my plum blossom: we
pledge ourselves.
A caress like two or three stalks of Yao grass,
She makes love like a graceful river nymph.
This feeling night after night: the sapphire sea, the
azure sky.

> IKKYU
> "Jonquil"

~

I drink streamwater and the air
becomes clearer and everything I do.

I become a waterwheel,
turning and tasting you, as long
as water moves.

> RUMI

A sage once advised, "Share not only your body, but your mind as well." Nowhere is this more true than in sharing sexual fantasies. Sometimes we are ashamed of our fantasies and therefore don't divulge them. But silence creates barriers and if we remain silent, we can find ourselves making love to some picture in our heads instead of the person next to us in the bed.

Don't shut your lover out. Let him or her know your fantasies so he or she can be included. If it's too difficult for you to speak, try writing him or her a note of what you would like to do. Perhaps you can even take turns enacting one another's fantasies.

The men long for their women. Often in the night the dark barn suddenly becomes warm with familiar scents and breezes, embracing me from an imaginary, distant savannah, springing like an ambuscade off the river Kalwara. I am home, I think. My eyes roam the farthest recesses and a slim figure, her naked form perfectly outlined in the moonlight, always approaches me. She glows like a firefly, her breath a haze in the smoky air. Dazed but not alarmed, I rise and follow her, stumbling amongst the mattresses of the other men. I reach an opening, an unequal circle that pierces the tangled undergrowth of a riverbank. The circle's moss is soft underfoot and spongy, and the crystal river swallows us both silently. I slide under her floating form, my arms embracing the wetness of the palm-oiled flesh, my hands groping her dark triangle and her illuminated breasts, which break the surface like tiny pyramids. Her thousand plaits fan out around her head, the multicolored cowrie shells reflecting the moonlight. Her lynx eyes open and her breath laps my face as she twists over, half swimming away. But I always catch the weightless body and carry her downstream, caressing her limbs, flanks, thorax, as she turns and turns in my arms. I dive under the surface, taking her with me, and plunge into her rotating body, carried even deeper by the tepid undertow. The current always runs counter to our movements, and we struggle down to the slimy bottom, locking and unlocking in violent spasms until, with a sigh, she releases me and all of me flees into her nest, my snake reaching her innermost parts, commanding both our cries of pleasure at the same time, while her body still swivels in my arms. I enter her again, churning the turbid waters as we grasp and ungrasp like wrestlers, her arms above her head, her body bent like a bow, her breath whistling through her, love kisses and cries that split the air as we rock, locked in an arc, still in motion, sinking onto the bed of the river shimmering with filtered moonlight. Rushing downward blindly, her body smashes against mine, I burst inside her, a roaring in my ears as my throat explodes with her name.

BARBARA CHASE RIBOUD
from *Echo of Lions*

Ecstatic
Destinations

"Making love is the interface of the physical
and the spiritual, the mortal and the immortal.
Making love is the balm and the bond, the
giving and the gift."

DAPHNE ROSE KINGMA

$\mathcal{S}$unday morning may be the only time during the week that you can approach lovemaking completely relaxed, perhaps bringing with you some faint memories of dreams, but no stresses and anxieties. Everyone else is sleeping in, too. This is the only morning that you're unlikely to be disturbed by the ringing of the telephone. Make the most of it. Take this opportunity to make love in the daylight.

It may take courage. Some of you may have to deal with feelings of embarrassment—rarely does anyone consider his or her own body to be perfect. Candlelight is flattering, while darkness covers a multitude of flaws. Everything can be seen in the light of day. Making love in the daytime can be a real test for lovers who have been living in illusion. In the Bible, having sex was called "knowing" someone, and it was a good word to use—being able to see what you're doing clearly means you will know and be known in truth. Daytime sex is just one more step toward pulling down barriers so that you and your lover can be truly united.

ZSUZSANNA E. BUDAPEST
The Goddess in the Bedroom

*L*overs, gratified in each other, I am asking *you*
about us. You hold each other. Where is your proof?
Look, sometimes I find that my hands have become
aware of each other, or that my time-worn face
shelters itself inside them. That gives me a slight
sensation. But who would dare to exist, just for that?
You, though, who in each other's passion
grow until, overwhelmed, he begs you:

"No *more* . . ."; you who beneath his hands
swell with abundance, like autumn grapes;
you who may disappear because the other has wholly
emerged: I am asking *you* about us. I know,
you touch so blissfully because the caress preserves,
because the place you so tenderly cover does not
vanish; because underneath it you feel pure duration.
So you promise eternity, almost, from the embrace.
    And yet, when you have survived the terror of the
first glances, the longing at the window, and the first
walk together, once only, through the garden:

lovers, *are* you the same? When you lift yourselves up
to each other's mouth and your lips join, drink against
drink:

oh how strangely each drinker seeps away from his
action.

Weren't you astonished by the caution of human
gestures on Attic gravestones? Wasn't love and depar-
ture placed so gently on shoulders that it seemed to be
made of a different substance than in our world?
Remember the hands, how weightlessly they rest,
though there is power in the torsos.

These self-mastered figures know: "We can go this far,
this is ours, to touch one another this lightly; the gods
can press down harder upon us. But that is the gods'
affair."

> RAINER MARIA RILKE
> from *The Second Duino Elegy*
> translated by Stephen Mitchell

161

$\mathscr{A}$t night, when you were in my body, when you were the tree giving breath to the night, I took it in. We lay there, your mouth open against mine with the breath going back and forth. I said, "This is the Amazon. I want to grow dark as a jungle with you, to feed all the myriad birds, to give off air to breathe." We lay together, dark woods feeding the universe, you breathing into me; I, taking your breath, holding it in my body, saying, "Life, Life, Life."

I wanted to be a plant form. I wanted to laugh under you like grass, to bend and ripple, to be the crisp smell, to be so common about you, to be everywhere about you, to house the small and be there under your body when you rolled there, where I was.

I wanted to be the animal form. I wanted to howl, to speak the moon language, to rut with you as the August moon tipped toward roundness and the blood poured out of my body. I held your penis that had plunged into me, and afterwards my hands were red with my own blood. I wanted to paint our faces, to darken our mouths, to make the mark of blood across our bodies, to write "Life, Life, Life" in the goat smell of your hands. You carried it all day on your fingers, as

I carried your pulse in my swollen cunt, the beat
repeating itself like a heart. My body had shaped itself
to yours, was opening and closing.

I wanted to be the forms of light, to be the wind,
the vision, to burn you like a star, to wrap you in
storm, to make the tree yield. I wanted to drown in
your white water, and where your fingers probed I
wanted to hear each pore cry out, "Open, Open. Break
Open! Let nothing be hidden or closed."

I wanted to be all the violences opening, all earth-
quake and avalanche, and the quiet, all the dawns and
dusks, all the deep blues of my body, the closing and
opening of light. I wanted to be the breath from the
lungs of the universe, and to open your mouth with a
tongue of rain, to touch all the corners and joinings.
And when you entered me, when I heard you cry,
"Love me, love me, love me with your mouth," I
wanted to enter you with everything wet and fiery, to
enter you with breath until you also called out and
called out and called out, "Life, Life, Life."

DEENA METZGER
"The Work to Know What Life Is"

163

5.

then I take my tongue to your body
letting it wander blind over your ribs
as if each were one string of a harp
leaving no string untouched

we reach our hands deep into one another
and if they come up at all
they come up full of poetry the moon
a few stars and a silence rinsed in blood

who dares speak against that silence
let him speak

I have loved you honestly
with all my crooked heart and gently
as darkness comes to water
and in passion with the storm

of all the nothings I have ever said
one word remains
I wear it as a wafer on my tongue
it is your name

6.

bind up the sagging breasts of morning
oh my darling let the light in

your hair is more beautiful than dawn

we have arrived years later
at the starting place
now we shall begin again

> RICHARD SHELTON
> from "The Fourteenth Anniversary"

*H*is room was like a traveler's den, full of objects from all over the world. The walls were covered with red rugs, the bed was covered with animal furs. The place was close, intimate, voluptuous like the rooms of an opium dream. The furs, the deep-red walls, the objects, like the fetishes of an African priest—everything was violently erotic. I wanted to lie naked on the furs, to be taken there lying on this animal smell, caressed by the fur.

I stood there in the red room, and Marcel undressed me. He held my naked waist in his hands. He eagerly explored my body with his hands. He felt the strong fullness of my hips.

"For the first time, a real woman," he said. "So many have come here, but for the first time here is a real woman, someone I can worship."

As I lay on the bed it seemed to me that the smell and feel of the fur and the bestiality of Marcel were combined. Jealousy had broken his timidity. He was like an animal, hungry for every sensation, for every way of knowing me. He kissed me eagerly, he bit my lips. He lay in the animal furs, kissing my breasts, feeling my legs, my sex, my buttocks. Then in the half-light he moved up over me, shoving his penis in my mouth. I felt my teeth catching on it as he pushed it inand out, but he liked it. He was watching and caressing me, his hands all over my body, his fingers everywhere seeking to know me completely, to hold me.

I threw my legs up over his shoulders high, so that he could plunge into me and see it at the same time. He wanted to see everything. He wanted to see how the penis went in and came out glistening and firm, big. I held myself up on my two fists so as to offer my sex more and more to his thrusts. Then he turned me over and lay over me like a dog, pushing his penis in from behind, with his hands cupping my breasts, caressing me and pushing me at the same time. He was untiring. He would not come. I was waiting to have the orgasm with him, but he postponed and postponed it. He wanted to linger, to feel my body forever, to be endlessly excited. I was growing tired and I cried out, 'Come now, Marcel, come now.' He began then to push violently, moving with me into the wild rising peak of the orgasm, and then I cried out, and he came almost at the same time. We fell back among the furs, released.

ANAÏS NIN

THE LOVER: You were telling me a story
THE WOMAN: About the mermaid.

*S*he smoothes his skin running her hands down his hips onto his thighs, avoiding the center of his belly and his groin, smoothing down the skin turning opalescent under her fingers, the scales forming where she strokes him—thin, delicate armor, sharp; transparent petals, layered one on the other. The water follows her unimpeded, the scales directing the rivulets toward deepening pools. His feet join at the ankles, the toes thin and spread. The bones dissolve. Fins or seaweed emerge where his feet were. The bed is water. They absorb the common motion of the currents. Wherever she touches him, he alters. "I have always dreamed you this way," she says.

And at the waist, her flesh midriff against his chest, still flesh, her breasts against his nipples, their mouths make the fish, her hair carried damply across his face, the sweat is cool as sea water, they thrash about each other. Her skin glistens and his hands follow the light but that her tail slashes and the spray covers them. He enters where he can enter. Her mouth like the whale opens for what small fish will winnow through her teeth. When the jaw clenches behind, the probing finger can open it, and he jumps into the cavernous body across the pink ribs and into the salt-reeking dark among the smooth creatures, the odor of surf, shells appointed to sand by the thunderous ocean tail, the open bones, plankton, sea horses, jelly fish, all the transparent wonders are there. He holds her fingers up to the light to see the blood in her, the smooth rope which ties her, the live girdle encircling her, which turns her to the creatures which move in the dark. Ink to close her eyes and more hands than she can count.

Now he bridles her. The little pods of kelp break in her mouth. The cold tails beat in the water and the white foam passes the seeds through their water bodies. "I dream you this way," she whispers, her eyes opening from under the tide.

"I would be a moray eel," he answers. "I am so voracious."

"And your colors, what colors are you?"

He puts his fingers on her eyes and closes them. "Can you see," he strokes her, "the colors only the dark knows?" He slides into her, one fish opening its mouth and the other entering, this constant devouring; he is whole within her and yet he holds her. The beating tails keep them afloat; she extends to the shape he assumes, the tails flutter, and the spindrift catches them, tossing them whitely.

"You are more ravenous than I." Still he emerges unmarred. The tide pools are gentle. The anemones close or open to the sun.

DEENA METZGER
from *The Woman Who Slept with Men to Take the War Out of Them*

~

The best sex comes not from doing but from *allowing*—allowing the sexual energy between you to move as it desires. The best sex is like surfing; you go with the current. It's not like driving a tractor, it's more like riding a surfboard. You can influence the outcome by swaying a little here and swaying a little there, but you can't force anything. If you don't love the tides—well, the tides are much stronger than you can ever be, and if you don't love them and respect them, surfing will very quickly become a nightmare.

WILLIAM ASHOKA ROSS

I wanna call you all the names, baby honey, sweet love, darling, sugarpie, rosehips, apricot lips, I wanna laugh so it's so far down in my belly you feel it through your lovable dick up through your groin until your epiglottis wags with joy, hey honey, don't need no lunch when I got you, don't need no bath, the odors we let out has them formin lines to see what we hot cookin, everything comin out of our kitchen, hot and earthy stew, epicurean souffle, long island duckling even, give me your leg, you take the delicate rise near my breast, this is the first of May and if it wasn't rainin so hard, we'd be lovin it up under that tree, you know the one with the fingers on the ground and the whole earth'd be pushin up against that perfect ass of yours, pine needles stickin in your crack, smells we'd longed for all the winter, dirt on my knees, worms wonderin what the fuss is overhead, everything steamy as if an eruption were imminent, our mouths busy planting and in out heads, the crops, corn, alfalfa, jungles of beans applauding our recognition of the day.

JUDITH W. STEINBERGH
"May Day"

171

𝒰sing your tongue during sex is an art. A woman knows instantly when her lover is enjoying giving her pleasure. Men report they value oral sex highly. Your partner would enjoy having you go down on him, too, and he hopes that you find it pleasurable. It is said that when a man goes down on a woman, he can achieve an erection and maintain it longer. Having oral sex performed on you is an acceptance of your secret, animal self and an absolute must if you're allowing someone into your body. If you enjoy what your lover is doing, let him or her know. Moan. Run your hands through his hair. Push his or her head into you. Create a harmony with your movements. Imagine this as a long-lasting activity with no ultimate goal. Time is suspended. Explore each other. Enjoy each other. Take time, and pause for a little while if you feel like it. You might come this way, you might not. She or he might come, or might not. If something happens that's funny, take a break and laugh. Among the Eskimo, making love is called *laughing together.* Remember to be light-hearted and playful when making love.

ZSUZSANNA E. BUDAPEST
The Goddess in the Bedroom

$\mathcal{L}$overs in their play—when they have liberated from the traditions which bound them to the trivial or the gross conception of play in love—are thus moving amongst the highest human activities, alike of the body and of the soul. They are passing to each other the sacramental chalice of that wine which imparts the deepest joy that men and women can know. They are subtly weaving the invisible cords that bind husband and wife together more truly and more firmly than the priest of any church. And if in the end—as may or may not be—they attain the climax of free and complete union, then their human play has become one with that divine play of creation in which old poets fabled that, out of the dust of the ground and in his own image, some God of Chaos once created Man.

HAVELOCK ELLIS

173

When I was a connoisseuse of slugs
I would part the ivy leaves, and look for the
naked jelly of those gold bodies,
translucent strangers glistening along the
stones, slowly, their gelatinous bodies
at my mercy. Made mostly of water, they would shrivel
to nothing if they were sprinkled with salt,
but I was not interested in that. What I liked
was to draw aside the ivy, breathe the
odor of the wall, and stand there in silence
until the slug forgot I was there
and sent its antennae up out of its
head, the glimmering umber horns
rising like telescopes, until finally the
sensitive knobs would pop out the ends,
delicate and intimate. Years later,
when I first saw a naked man,
I gasped with pleasure to see that quiet
mystery reenacted, the slow
elegant being coming out of hiding and
gleaming in the dark air, eager and so
trusting you could weep.

SHARON OLDS
"The Connoisseuse of Slugs"

The night we missed the boat at Algeciras the
watchman going about serene with his lamp and O
that awful deepdown torrent O and the sea the sea
crimson sometimes like fire and the glorious sunsets
and the figtrees in the Alameda gardens yes and all the
queer little streets and pink and blue and yellow
houses and the rosegardens and the jessamine and
geraniums and cactuses and Gibraltar as a girl where I
was a Flower of the mountain yes when I put the rose in
my hair like the Andalusian girls used or shall I wear a
red yes and how he kissed me under the Moorish wall
and I thought well as well him as another and then I
asked him with my eyes to ask again yes and then he
asked me would I say yes my mountain flower and first
I put my arms around him yes and drew him down to
me so he could feel my breasts all perfume yes and his
heart was going like mad and yes I said yes I will Yes.

JAMES JOYCE
from *Ulysses*

175

$\mathcal{D}$o you remember the time you had that perfect orgasm? The one you and your partner reminisce about? The golden screw? Everyone who's ever had it always wants to reexperience it. And when we can't, we feel frustrated because none of our efforts work— and we of course feel they *should* work!

Some people think that's why it doesn't happen anymore—because we're trying to repeat, to copy, to imitate. If, instead of trying to recapture the past, we could be open to the brand new, to *all* the newness and freshness and awe that life has to offer, who knows what wonderful experiences might come our way?

WILLIAM ASHOKA ROSS

~

$\mathcal{W}$hat is erotic? The acrobatic play of the imagination. The sea of memories in which we bathe. The way we caress and worship things with our eyes. Our willing- ness to be stirred by the sight of the voluptuous. What is erotic is our passion for the liveliness of life.

DIANE ACKERMAN

From pent-up aching rivers,
From that of myself without which I were nothing,
From what I am determin'd to make illustrious, even if
    I stand sole
among men,
From my own voice resonant, singing the phallus,
Singing the song of procreation,
Singing the need of superb children and therein superb
    grown
people,
Singing the muscular urge and the blending,
Singing the bedfellow's song, (O resistless yearning!
O for any and each the body correlative attracting!
O for you whoever you are your correlative body! O it,
    more than all else, you delighting!)
From the hungry gnaw that eats me night and day,
From native moments, from bashful pains, singing
    them,
Seeking something yet unfound though I have dili-
    gently sought it
many a long year,
Singing the true song of the soul fitful at random,
Renascent with grossest Nature or among animals,
Of that, of them and what goes with them my poems
    informing,

177

Of the smell of apples and lemons, of the pairing of
    birds,
Of the wet of woods, of the lapping of waves,
Of the mad pushes of waves upon the land, I them
    chanting,
The overture lightly sounding, the strain anticipating,
The welcome nearness, the sight of the perfect body,
The swimmer swimming naked in the bath, or motion-
    less on his
back lying and floating,
The female form approaching, I pensive, love-flesh
    tremulous
aching,
The divine list for myself or you or for any one making,
The face, the limbs, the index from head to foot, and
    what it
arouses,
The mystic deliria, the madness amourous, the utter
    abandonment,
(Hark close and still what I now whisper to you,
I love you, O you entirely possess me,
O that you and I escape from the rest and go utterly
    off, free and
lawless,
Two hawks in the air, two fishes swimming in the sea
    not more
lawless than we;)

The furious storm through me careering, I passionately
    trembling,
The oath of the inseparableness of two together, of the
    woman that
loves me and whom I love more than my life, that oath
swearing,
(O I willingly stake all for you,
O let me be lost if it must be so!
O you and I! what is it to us what the rest do or think?
What is all else to us? Only that we enjoy each other
    and exhaust
each other if it must be so;)
From the master, the pilot I yield the vessel to,
The general commanding me, commanding all, from
    him permission taking,
From time the programme hastening, (I have loiter'd
    too long as it
is,)
From sex, from the warp and from the woof,
From privacy, from frequent repinings alone,
From plenty of persons near and yet the right person
    not near,
From the soft sliding of hands over me and thrusting of
    fingers
through my hair and beard,

From the long sustain'd kiss upon the mouth or bosom,
From the close pressure that makes me or any man
    drunk, fainting with excess,
From what the divine husband knows, from the work
    of father-hood,
From exultation, victory and relief from the bedfellow's
    embrace in
the night,
From the act-poems of eyes, hands, hips and bosoms,
From the cling of the trembling arm,
From the bending curve and the clinch,
From side by side the pliant coverlet off-throwing,
From the one so unwilling to have me leave, and me
    just as unwilling to leave,
(Yet a moment O tender waiter, and I return,)
From the hour of shining stars and dropping dews,
From the night a moment I emerging flitting out,
Celebrate your act divine and your children prepared
    for,
And you shall stalwart loins.

                    WALT WHITMAN
                    "From Pent-Up Aching Rivers"

$\mathcal{D}$o you know how to talk to her body until it opens for you like a flower? Do you know how to tell him how much you want him until he swells with desire?

There is a time during sexual lovemaking for silence, and there is also a time for words. Words add a whole other dimension to lovemaking. They create yet another channel across which your love can flow. While the movement of your body and the sounds you make communicate to your partner's body, *words communicate your passion to your lover's brain.* And it's the brain that controls all the pleasure centers in your body.

BARBARA DE ANGELIS

So it is with life, and especially with love. There is no point. There is nothing you can cut out, except falsity, which isn't love or life. But the love itself is a flow, two little streams of feeling, one from the woman, one from the man, that flow and flow and never stop, and sometimes they twinkle with stars, sometimes they chafe, but still they flow on, intermingling; and if they rise to a floweriness like a daisy, that is part of the flow; and they will inevitably die down again, which is also part of a flow. And one relationship may produce many flowerinesses, as a daisy plant produces many daisies; but they will all die down again as the summer passes, though the green plant itself need not die. If flowers didn't fade they wouldn't be flowers, they'd be artificial things. But there are roots to faded flowers and in the root the flow continues and continues. And only the flow matters; live and let live, love and let love. There is no point to love.

D. H. LAWRENCE

She swung her leg across his chest and, bending, took him in her mouth. The sensation of her sucking at him, and her hair dancing on his thighs as she rocked to and fro, was almost unbearable in its intensity.

He raised his head. Her sex was like a delicate sea shell, the palest pink fading into white. It opened each time she rocked forward, while above her buttocks parted and disclosed a tiny pink rose.

He groaned as she took him deeper in her mouth, moving more urgently. The pleasure began like a thrill deep inside him, rising nearer and nearer to the surface . . . At last it was released. That was the crisis of his pleasure, that and her soft mouth sucking the pumping shaft and drinking him.

She kissed him slowly on the lips. Her breath was like new mown grass. 'I love the taste of you.'

excerpt from *Passion's Apprentice*

183

And timorously, his hands went over her, over the salt, compact brilliance of her body. If he could but have her, how he would enjoy her! If he could but net her brilliant, cold, slat-burning body in the soft iron of his own hands, net her, capture her, hold her down, how madly he would enjoy her. He strove subtly, but with all his energy, to enclose her, to have her. And always she was burning and brilliant and hard as salt, and deadly. Yet obstinately, all his flesh burning and corroding, as if he were invaded by some consuming, scathing poison, still he persisted, thinking at last he might overcome her. Even, in his frenzy, he sought for her mouth with his mouth, though it was like putting his face into some awful death. She yielded to him, and he pressed himself upon her in extremity, his soul groaning over and over:

'Let me come—let me come.'

She took him in the kiss, hard her kiss seized upon him, hard and fierce and burning corrosive as the moonlight. She seemed to be destroying him. He was reeling, summoning all his strength to keep his kiss upon her, to keep himself in the kiss.

But hard and fierce she had fastened upon him, cold as the moon and burning as a fierce salt. Till gradually his warm, soft iron yielded, yielded, and she was there fierce, corrosive, seething with his destruction, seething like some cruel, corrosive salt around the last substance of his being, destroying him, destroying him in the kiss. And her soul crystallized with triumph, and his soul was dissolved with agony and annihilation. So she held him there, the victim, consumed, annihilated. She had triumphed: he was not any more.

D. H. LAWRENCE
from *The Rainbow*

~

When you came, you were like red wine and honey,
And the taste of you burnt my mouth with its sweetness.
Now you are like morning bread,
Smooth and pleasant.
I hardly taste you at all for I know your savour,
But I am completely nourished.

AMY LOWELL
"A Decade"

Speak earth and bless me
with what is richest
make sky flow honey out of my hips
rigid as mountains
spread over a valley
carved out by the mouth of rain.

And I knew when I entered her   I was
high wind in her forest's hollow
fingers whispering sound
honey flowed   from the split cup
impaled on a lance of tongues
on the tips of her breasts on her navel
and my breath   howling into her entrances
through lungs of pain.

Greedy as herring-gulls
or a child
I swing out over the earth
over and over   again.

AUDRE LORDE
"Love Poem"

$\mathcal{I}$n sexual ecstasy your boundaries disappear. Your heart opens out like a great sail as your vital force mingles with that of your beloved. Your body no longer feels solid; you become pulsating energy instead. There are physicists who say that the universe is basically not matter but conscious energy. Ecstasy is a way of bathing yourself in that energy—a way of being rejuvenated with God.

Ecstatic orgasm is an electric, euphoric, tingling, sparkling experience; a moment suspended in time; a dark, pulsating sea of intense feeling; a quickening of the senses; a cataclysm; a gorgeous feeling of floating. Some report it "makes me feel weak and shaky and powerful all at the same time"; "cancels out all discontent"; "makes me hyper-sensitive all over"; "takes my breath away as it floods my body with dazzling sunshine." Some talk of an eternal now, of time standing still, of blinding flashes of light, of painful yet wonderful explosions of glowing warmth. Others experience being "completely in harmony with the universe" and "something from the beyond beckoning." Next to being born, giving birth, and dying, ecstasy is the most miraculous experience of all.

WILLIAM ASHOKA ROSS

$\mathcal{I}$'m touched by his awkward courtesy. Tilting forward, I tongue the sprinkling of hairs at the base of his penis, and at last he lets go of my head. I sink my mouth into the muscle of his inner thigh, wishing I could swallow him whole, but I only graze there before sliding up to his tight, high balls—I like it when a man's balls harden and lift, as sign of urgency—popping each one in my mouth like candy, and finally I begin to blow him in earnest: in a rhythm of rocking need, like gliding along some primitive totem in an act of ceremonial worship. Baby, slave, siren, my lips a vise to grip his cock—cock, I say to myself and the word is guilty pleasure, almost an act of thievery. I hear him gasping and I'm glad—a cruel euphoria—I'd like to see his face when he comes, see those spasms that look like grief, derangement, rage, but are pleasure. Still, I'm surprised when he begins to utter words, phrases that sound hackneyed to any ear, *god, oh god, woman, oh Christ*, except I'm crazy for those lonesome words, want to hear him call me woman a hundred times, not Lynn, not darling, not baby, but woman, woman. The whole length of him stiffens as I suck, whatever way I want, I'm merciless now, I—slow—down—, he pleads, I stop, his hands slip blindly over my face, I take him

all at once, half-choking but I manage it, until he
growls in pain like somebody dying alone in the night,
driving deeper than he should so I feel his penis bunting
the small cone of flesh that hangs from the back of my
throat, I'm pushing him away with my hands then
breathing and sucking him in again when suddenly he
cries *no*. And the *no* beats like drum-bursts under the
rhythm of need until he takes up the cry again, a
riotous, red-hot, convulsive cry he keeps hurling at me,
he cannot move or master himself, he's lost and he
loves it, and utters a low animal scream as his body
starts to buck, arching, and I hold him so he comes in
my hands.

JILL NEIMARK
from *Bloodsong*

Settle for
Settle for nothing
Settle for nothing less
Settle for nothing less than

Settle for nothing
less than the
object of your
desire.

Desire. The weight of. The weight of our
desire. Then laugh, cry, but laugh
more than you cry, and when you hold
the world in your hands, love Her.

ALMA LUZ VILLANUEVA
from "The Object"

She murmured, "Take your clothes off."

He undressed. Naked, he knew his power. He was more at ease naked than clothed because he had been an athlete, a swimmer, a walker, a mountain climber. And he knew then that he could please her.

She looked at him.

Was she pleased? When he bent over her, was she more responsive? He could not tell. By now he desired her so much that he could not wait to touch her with the tip of his sex, but she stopped him. She wanted to kiss and fondle it. She set about this with so much eagerness that he found himself with her full backside near his face and able to kiss and fondle her to his content.

By now he was taken with the desire to explore and touch every nook of her body. He parted the opening of her sex with his two fingers, he feasted his eyes on the glowing skin, the delicate flow of honey, the hair curling around his fingers. His mouth grew more and more avid, as if it had become a sex organ in

191

itself, capable of so enjoying her that if he continued to fondle her flesh with his tongue he would reach some absolutely unknown pleasure. As he bit into her flesh with such a delicious sensation, he felt again in her a quiver of pleasure. Now he forced her away from his sex, for fear she might experience all her pleasure merely kissing him and that he would be cheated of feeling himself inside of her womb. It was as if they both had become ravenously hungry for the taste of flesh. And now their two mouths melted into each other, seeking the leaping tongues.

Her blood was fired now. By his slowness he seemed to have done this, at last. Her eyes shone brilliantly, her mouth could not leave his body. And finally he took her, as she offered herself, opening her vulva with her lovely fingers, as if she could no longer wait. Even then they suspended their pleasure, and she felt him quietly, enclosed.

Then she pointed to the mirror and said, laughing, "Look, it appears as if we were not making love, as if I were merely sitting on your knees, and you, you rascal, you have had it inside me all the time, and you're even quivering. Ah, I can't bear it any longer, this pretending I have nothing inside. It's burning me up. Move now, move!"

She threw herself over him so that she could gyrate around his erect penis, deriving from this erotic dance a pleasure which made her cry out. And at the same time a lightning flash of ecstasy tore through George's body.

ANAÏS NIN

~

*Y*our face is the light in here that makes
my arms full of gentleness.
The beginning of a month-long holiday, the disc
of the full moon, the shade of your hair,
these draw me in. I dive
into the deep pool of a mountain river,
folded into union,
as the split-second when the bat meets the ball,
and there is one cry between us.

RUMI
"Folded Into the River"

193

I see a horse and trap drawn up by the front door of the farmhouse. In it is a man in black with a bowler hat. He is portly and unaccountably comic. The horse is black and so too is the trap except for its white trimming. I am looking down on the horse and trap and the man who is so comically correct and regular, from the window of Beatrice's room.

On the table between the window and the large four-poster bed is the vase of white lilac. The smell of it is the only element that I can reconstruct with certainty.

She must be thirty-six. Her hair, usually combed up into a chignon, is loose around her shoulders. She wears an embroidered wrap. The embroidered leaves mount to her shoulder. She is standing in bare feet.

The boy enters and informs her that the papers for the man in the trap were the correct ones.

He is fifteen: taller than Beatrice, dark-haired, large-nosed but with delicate hands, scarcely larger than hers. In the relation between his head and shoulders there is something of his father—a kind of lunging assurance.

Beatrice lifts an arm towards him and opens her hand.

Pushing the door shut behind him, he goes towards her and takes her hand.

She, by turning their hands, ensures that they both look out of the window. At the sight of the man in black on the point of leaving they begin to laugh.

When they laugh they swing back the arms of their held hands and this swinging moves them away from the window towards the bed.

They sit on the edge of the bed before they stop laughing.

Slowly they lie back until their heads touch the counterpane. In this movement backwards she slightly anticipates him.

They are aware of a taste of sweetness in their throats. (A sweetness not unlike that to be tasted in a sweet grape.) The sweetness itself is not extreme but the experience of tasting it is. It is comparable with the experience of acute pain. But whereas pain closes anticipation of everything except the return of the past before the pain existed, what is now desired has never existed.

From the moment he entered the room it has been as though the sequence of their actions constituted a single act, a single stroke.

195

Beatrice puts her hand to the back of his head to move him closer towards her.

Beneath her wrap Beatrice's skin is softer than anything he has previously imagined. He has thought of softness as a quality belonging either to something small and concentrated (like a peach) or else to something extensive but thin (like milk). Her softness belongs to a body which has substance and seems very large. Not large relative to him, but large relative to anything else he now perceives. This magnification of her body is partly the result of proximity and focus but also of the sense of touch superseding that of sight. She is no longer contained within any contour, she is continuous surface.

He bends his head to kiss her breast and take the nipple in his mouth. His awareness of what he is doing certifies the death of his childhood. This awareness is inseparable from a sensation and a taste in his mouth. The sensation is of a morsel, alive, unaccountably half-detached from the roundness of the breast—as though it were on a stalk. The taste is so associated with the texture and substance of the morsel and with its temperature, that it will be hard ever to define it in other terms. It is a little similar to the taste of the whitish juice in the stem of a certain kind of grass. He is aware that henceforth both sensation and taste are acquirable on his own initiative. Her breasts propose his independence. He buries his face between them.

Her difference from him acts like a mirror. Whatever he notices or dwells upon in her, increases his consciousness of himself, without his attention shifting from her. . .

He hears the voice of an unknown woman speaking to him: Sweet, sweet, sweetest. Let us go to that place.

He unhesitatingly puts his hand on her hair and opens his fingers to let it spring up between them. What he feels in his hand is inexplicably familiar.

She opens her legs. He pushes his finger towards her. Warm mucus encloses his finger as closely as if it were a ninth skin. When he moves the finger, the surface of the enclosing liquid is stretched—sometimes to the breaking point. Where the break occurs he has a sensation of coolness on that side of his finger— before the warm moist skin forms again over the break.

She holds his penis with both hands, as though it were a bottle from which she were about to pour towards herself.

She moves sideways so as to be beneath him.

Her cunt begins at her toes; her breasts are inside it, and her eyes too; it has enfolded her.

It enfolds him.

The ease.

Previously it was unimaginable, like a birth for that which is born.

JOHN BERGER
excerpt from G

~

Tantric teachers Caroline and Charles Muir make the following suggestions for more meaningful lovemaking:

- Keep your eyes open as much as possible.
- Be love- and nurture-oriented rather than orgasm- performance-, or goal-oriented.
- It is blessed to give and receive. Make sure you are doing both.
- Remember to make Love a dance.

Body of a woman, white hills, white thighs,
you look like a world, lying in surrender.
My rough peasant's body digs in you
and makes the son leap from the depth of the earth.

I only was a tunnel. The birds fled from me,
and night swamped me with its crushing invasion.
To survive myself I forged you like a weapon,
like an arrow in my bow, a stone in my sling.

But the hour of vengeance falls, and I love you.
Body of skin, of moss, of eager and firm milk.
Oh the goblets of the breast! Oh the eyes of absence!
Oh the roses of the pubis! Oh your voice, slow and sad!

Body of my woman, I will persist in your grace.
My thirst, my boundless desire, my shifting road.
Dark river-beds where the eternal thirst flows
and weariness follows, and the infinite ache.

PABLO NERUDA
"Body of a Woman"

That day you seemed to me a tall palm tree
and your breasts
the clusters of its fruit.

I said in my heart,
Let me climb into that palm tree
and take hold of its branches.

And oh, may your breasts be like clusters
of grapes on a vine, the scent
of your breath like apricots,
your mouth good wine—

That pleases my lover, rousing him
even from sleep.

I am my lover's,
he longs for me,
only for me.

> from *The Song of Songs*
> translated by Ariel Bloch
> and Chana Bloch

My wife insists on watching me fillet the fish I catch. She brings her lawn chair out back while I hose the concrete slab I use to clean them on. She watches me intently, making sure to say how good I am with knives, how easy I separate the flesh from bone and slice the skin away. She likes for me to open up their stomachs and pull the contents out[m]half-digested crayfish, minnows, bugs, bait, and even plastic worms. If the stomach is empty, she tells me to turn it inside out so she can see the ridges which, to her, look like a brain. When I finish one, I hand her the fillets. She sprays them off, lightly, so they won't tear, and leaning down so I can see her cleavage, places them in the bucket. Then she fills its, swirls the water with her free hand, and talks to the fillets, telling them how nice they are, telling them to swim. She is serious, all the while looking straight at them and chanting her words. She gets sexier as she goes. By the time I finish, her cheeks flush and burn, but I just go about my business like nothing's happening. I watch her pull fillet after fillet from the bucket and shake each one until it's dry enough to carry in the house. I bury all the bones and guts and skin and take my time cleaning off the slab and putting up my gear, placing my rods along the cellar wall and straightening my tackle boxes. I smoke a couple cigarettes and close the cellar door behind me when I leave. The house is silent when I enter. The first uncooked fillet rests on a plate smack in the middle of our foyer, and next to it, her shoes. I take the plate and follow her nylons up the stairs to the second plate. Two fillets, her blouse. I pile the fish on my plate. Down the hall, three fillets, her skirt. I pile the fish. The final plate's outside our bedroom door. Four filets and her favorite lace panties. By now I'm sure she knows I'm standing here. She starts to coo and rustle on our bed while I kneel down and heap the last fillets on my full plate. I touch her panties, feel the moisture soothe my fingertips, and rub my nails back and forth against the door as gently as I can. She gets louder and wilder. I crack the door enough to watch her work. Her hands are skimming across her breasts, rippling her skin like wind over water. I feel faint and almost drop from excitement. Holding my plate, I swing the door wide open with my foot. I stare, I gawk,

I ogle over her until she calls me in. I go to her and set the heaping plate between her legs. My clothes are sticking to my skin. I itch. She strips the top fillet from the pile, draws it down one leg, up the other, up her stomach, around her breasts, her shoulders, and her neck, brings the meat to her mouth, kisses it, and licks it clean. It glistens in her hand. She puts it back and I lift the plate and put it on the floor. I fake a cast, pretend to bump an orange Salty Craw across the bed. She doesn't hit. I fake a cast and touch her with my hand. She quivers once and strikes so hard I think my arm will snap. I pull back hard and try to horse her home, but she won't come that easily. I have to work my way around the bed while she, with her hands around my wrist, rolls back and forth. When she's tuckered out, I pull that slick and gorgeous trophy in and look at her. She sighs a little, so I ask her what I ought to do with her. Now I've caught her, now she's mine. I grab her by the arms, holding them tight enough to settle her. I make her answer me. She says, *I'll do you favors if you let me go. Like what,* I say, and watch the color rising on her chest. She says she'll fan my spawning bed with her tail and keep the bluegill

and the crayfish out. I tell her that's not good enough.
She breathes in deeply and then it comes: she offers to
fulfill my wildest dreams. I start to tell her that I love
her, but she's all over me in nothing flat. Her mouth's
on mine, and I can taste the fish she licked a little
while ago. She pulls my T-shirt up above my head and
yanks it off. And soon enough I'm naked to the bone.
She says I've got the kind of worm she needs and takes
me in her mouth. I fall back on the bed and tell her
what a fish she is. She keeps on going, bobbing her
head, tweeting it until I'm ready to scream. And then
she stops. *I want to spawn*, she says, climbing up beside
me. I let her roll on top of me and tell me that she's
lonely, that sexy fish like her are really sad and spend
their days swimming by themselves in all the darkest
coves which they can find. I kiss her neck and squeeze
her to me. She kisses back. I tell her now, for real, that
I'll swim with her through anything the years throw at
us, through weather bad and good, through indifferent
days and months when the whole sky is gray and
overcast with doubt. I tell her that I love her, that I
wouldn't let her swim alone through this lake's dark
and tangled coves. We taste each other's grit and
decide to go do it in the tub. We bring the plate and
set it on the sink top just for luck, then turn the

shower on and step in the tub. I grab a bar of soap and lather her down until she's slicker than a channel cat. She does the same for me, and we rub up against each other in the rising steam and let out lather mix like fish spunk as it swirls down our legs and drains away. Moaning like catfish, our bodies quaking, she lets me work my way into her. We go until we're spent and tangled together against the bathroom wall. The closest hand will shut the water off, and we will come apart eventually. But its good to stand here, flesh to flesh, where we'll come clean in the easy water and make a plan for how to cook the fish. Maybe we'll bake or fry or broil it, serve it with a garden salad, potatoes, fresh beans, a bottle of chardonnay. I admit I like it spicy best of all because that's how I like to think of her: the way she tastes and feels, the way she moves when I come home and show her what I've caught.

BOB ZORDANI
"A Fish Story"

Index

Permission Acknowlegments

Bountiful thanks for permission to excerpt from the following works:

True Love by Daphne Rose Kingma. Copyright © 1991 by Daphne Rose Kingma. Reprinted by permission of Conari Press. *A Garland of Love* by Daphne Rose Kingma. Copyright © 1992 by Daphne Rose Kingma. Reprinted by permission of Conari Press. *Wonderful Little Sex Book* by William Ashoka Ross. Copyright © 1987 and 1992 by William Ashoka Ross. Reprinted by permission of Conari Press. Reprinted by permission of the publishers and the Trustees of Amherst College from *The Poems of Emily Dickinson*, Thomas H. Johnson, ed., Cambridge, Mass: The Belknap Press of Harvard University Press. Copyright © 1951, 1955, 1979, 1983 by the President and Fellows of Harvard College. "The Work to Know What Life Is" from *Erotic By Nature: A Celebration of Life, of Love and of Our Wonderful Bodies*, edited by David Steinberg. Copyright © 1988 by Deena Metzger. Reprinted by permission of the editor. "To Whom It May Concern" from *Erotic By Nature: A Celebration of Life, of Love and of Our Wonderful Bodies*, edited by David Steinberg. Copyright © 1988 by David Steinberg. Reprinted by permission of the author. "Yellow Pears, Smooth as Silk" from *Erotic By Nature: A Celebration of Life, of Love and of Our Wonderful Bodies*, edited by David Steinberg. Copyright © 1975 by Rochelle Lynn Holt. Reprinted by permission of the editor. "The High Priestess" from *Erotic By Nature: A Celebration of Life, of Love and of Our Wonderful Bodies*, edited by David Steinberg. Copyright © 1988 by David Steinberg. Reprinted by permission of the author. "Witch/Song" from *Erotic By Nature: A Celebration of Life, of Love and of Our Wonderful Bodies*, edited by David Steinberg. Copyright © 1988 by Lenore Kandel. Reprinted by permission of the editor. "I Walk Out, Blindly" from *Erotic By Nature: A*

Conari Press, established in 1987, publishes books for women on topics ranging from spirituality and women's history, to sexuality and personal growth. Our main goal is to publish quality books that will make a difference in people's lives—both how we feel about ourselves and how we relate to one another.

Our readers are our most important resource, and we value your input, suggestions, and ideas. We'd love to hear from you—after all, we are publishing books for you!

For a complete catalog or to get on our mailing list, please contact us at:

CONARI PRESS

2550 Ninth Street, Suite 101
Berkeley, CA 94710
800-685-9595